HOW TO DO
PASTEUPS AND MECHANICALS

The Preparation of Art for Reproduction

HOW TO DO
PASTEUPS AND MECHANICALS

The Preparation of Art for Reproduction

By S. RALPH MAURELLO

Instructor and Executive Secretary,
Newark School of Fine and Industrial Art

Administrator, Old Mill Summer Art School
Elizabethtown, New York.

Author of:
Commercial Art Techniques
The Complete Airbrush Book

TUDOR PUBLISHING COMPANY

NEW YORK

MANUFACTURED IN THE UNITED STATES
BY GANIS AND HARRIS, NEW YORK

Dedicated to
"Spotty"
Who has a mind of her own.

TABLE OF CONTENTS

INTRODUCTION   IX

BASIC PROCEDURES   11

Mechanicals and Pasteups — Typical Mechanical — Equipment and Working Set-Up — Use of T-Square — Aligning the Paper — Use of Triangle.

CUTTING AND TRIMMING   25

Cutting — Sharpening Knives and Blades — Positioning Artwork — Cutting Flush Edges (Mortising).

PASTEUP METHODS   35

Use of Rubber Cement — Pasteup Procedures — Pasting Up Type — Combining Type, Photos, Art and Stats — Stripping-In Lettering.

SCALING AND CROPPING   47

Scaling — Scaling a Photo (Enlarging) — Scaling a Photo (Reducing) — Scaling (Irregular Shapes) — Tracing and Scaling Devices — Cropping and Scaling.

COMPOSITES   69

Making a Composite — Composite Plus Artwork — Pasteup with Borders — Pasteup Lettering — Application of Pasteup Lettering.

USE OF DRAFTING AND DRAWING INSTRUMENTS   101

Use of Ruling Pen — Drawing Circles — Drawing Ellipses — Angles, Degrees and Sectors — Duplicating an Angle — Ruling Straight Lines — Use of the French Curve — Dividing a Line.

PHOTOGRAPHS AND PHOTOSTATS   121

Photographic Procedures — Making a Photostat — Photographs — Photostats — Ordering Photostat Prints — Mounting Photo Prints — Photo Retouching — Spotting Prints — Making a Swab — Photo Retouching — Airbrushing a Background.

REPRODUCTION   135

Basic Principles — Photoengraving — Veloxes — Type.

COLOR SEPARATIONS   145

Color Separation Mechanical — Two-Color Mechanical (Line Art) — Mechanical Halftone and Solid, French-Fold — Mechanical Special Effects — Protecting Pasteups and Mechanicals.

GLOSSARY   160

INTRODUCTION

In advertising, publication and design fields, artwork is generally prepared for reproduction by the assemblage of various units of material. Such units may consist of type proofs, photostats, photographs, spot drawings, hand lettering, pasteup lettering, etc. These units are pasted in position, following a given layout; and additional art, such as ruling pen work, retouching, corrections, overlays, and drawing performed directly on the mechanical.

The term "Pasteups and Mechanicals" is generally applied to this type of artwork. This is the starting point for most artists entering the commercial art field, even though it may not be the type of work which the artist is most interested in, or most capable of doing. The artist may continue to do such work indefinitely, or, as is more usual, eventually move into some other category such as layout, lettering, design or illustration.

The actual practice of doing Pasteups and Mechanicals is generally not taught in schools, in spite of the fact that most studios, agencies and publishers expect beginners to know this type of work. Unfortunately, most art students are not even aware of the meaning of the term, let alone the practice, and do not realize its importance till they are asked to do the work, or see many ads for such positions. The author has been teaching this subject for several years as part of his Production Procedures course at the Newark School of Fine and Industrial Art, and is well aware of its importance in placing graduates.

While basically simple in execution, there are definite methods, terminology and procedures which must be used to assure accurate and reproducible art. It is the purpose of this book to provide such information completely and graphically enough to be learned from the instruction provided herein.

BASIC PROCEDURES

Fig. 1 Advertising Art

Mechanicals and Pasteups

Virtually all phases of advertising, editorial and graphic design utilize pasteups and mechanicals in their production stages. Illustrated here are some representational printed specimens which fall into this category; printed matter for which pasteups and mechanicals are utilized in the preparation of the original art. This by no means exhausts the range of material thus prepared, but represents some typical categories requiring mechanicals, varying from comparatively simple to rather complex treatment, involving color separation.

Fig. 2 Editorial Art

Fig. 3 Displays

Fig. 4 Letterheads

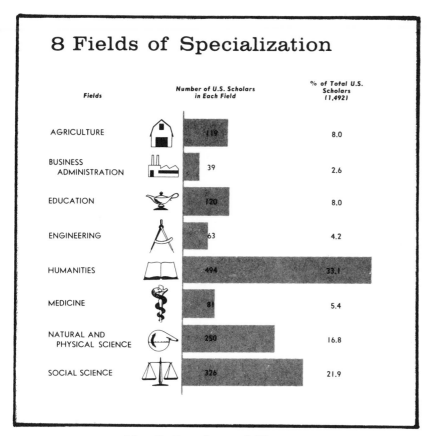

8 Fields of Specialization

Fields	Number of U.S. Scholars in Each Field	% of Total U.S. Scholars (1,492)
AGRICULTURE	119	8.0
BUSINESS ADMINISTRATION	39	2.6
EDUCATION	120	8.0
ENGINEERING	63	4.2
HUMANITIES	494	33.1
MEDICINE	81	5.4
NATURAL AND PHYSICAL SCIENCE	250	16.8
SOCIAL SCIENCE	326	21.9

Fig. 5 Graphs and Charts

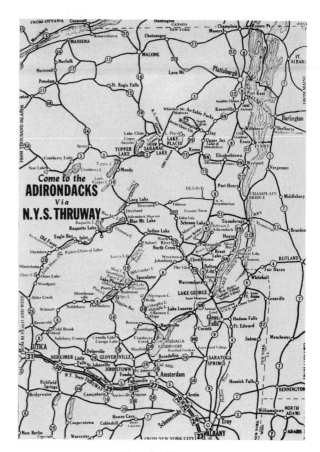

Fig. 6 Maps

On page 15 is a reproduction of a mechanical, as prepared for an actual job. Call-outs identify the various units for clarification in understanding the principles, procedures, techniques and instructions given in this book.

Fig. 7 Packaging

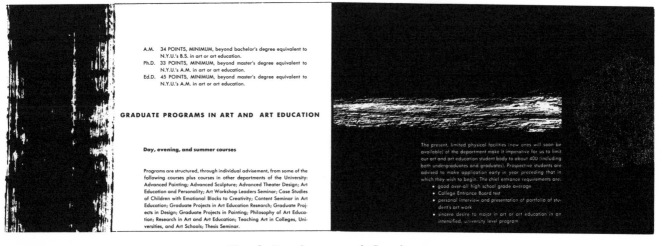

Fig. 8 Brochures and Catalogues

Typical Mechanical

On the opposite page is reproduced a typical mechanical, which was prepared for one side of the brochure shown on this page, FIG. 9, in its finished, printed form. The actual brochure is in two colors, a halftone black, with a solid pink background (printed here in flat gray). The mechanical represents the artwork for only the black halftone plate for one side of the brochure.

FIG. 10. For clarity in this book the background of the mechanical is shown as a light tone of gray, rather than its original white, so that the actual units of pasteup material can be more clearly identified. For the same reason the units are identified with "Call outs", which would not appear on the actual mechanical, though the *marks* identified, such as the trim and fold marks, do appear on the mechanical, along with any necessary directions for the engraver, such as for reversing type, etc.

A more complete explanation of this mechanical is given on page 150.

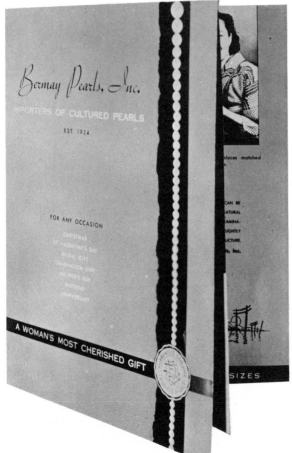

Fig. 9

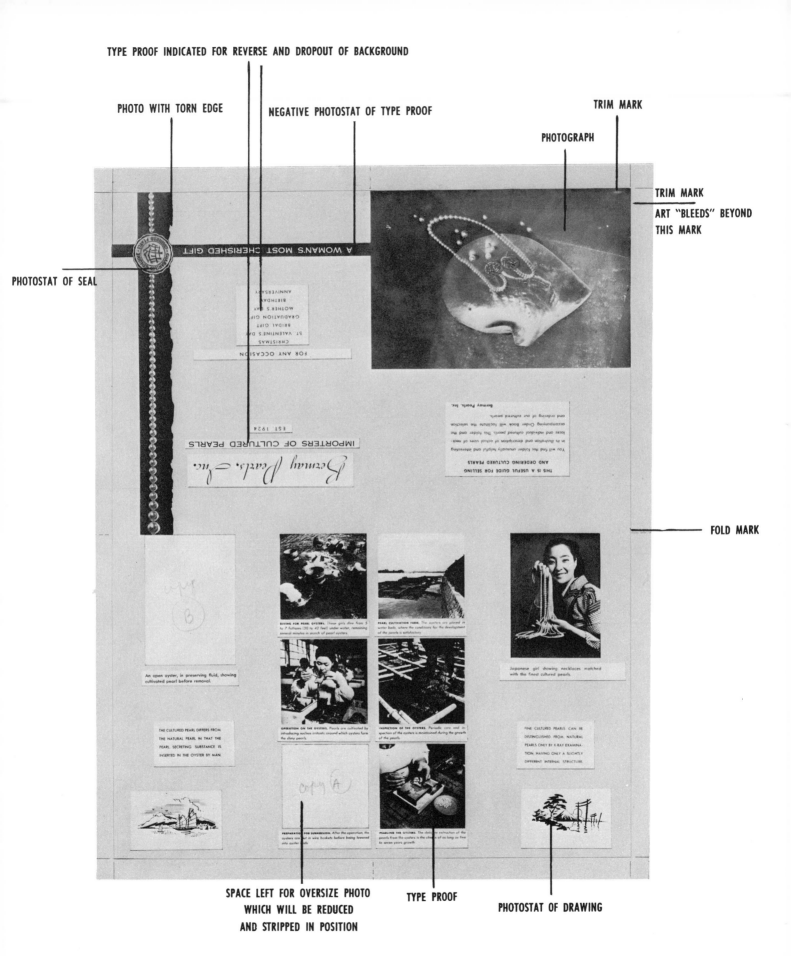

TYPE PROOF INDICATED FOR REVERSE AND DROPOUT OF BACKGROUND

PHOTO WITH TORN EDGE

NEGATIVE PHOTOSTAT OF TYPE PROOF

TRIM MARK

PHOTOGRAPH

TRIM MARK
ART "BLEEDS" BEYOND
THIS MARK

PHOTOSTAT OF SEAL

FOLD MARK

SPACE LEFT FOR OVERSIZE PHOTO
WHICH WILL BE REDUCED
AND STRIPPED IN POSITION

TYPE PROOF

PHOTOSTAT OF DRAWING

Fig. 10

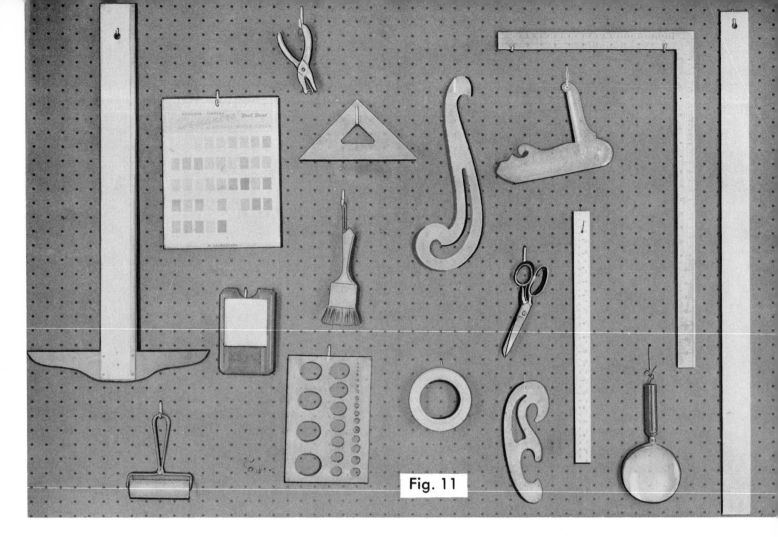

Fig. 11

Equipment and Working Set-Up

The work of the pasteup artist necessitates accuracy, precision and neatness. The tools and equipment are simple and few, but must be of good quality, carefully and properly used.

FIG. 11. *A peg-board panel* for hanging tools makes it convenient to replace them when not in use, and to locate them when wanted.

FIG. 13. *A single-pedestal drawing table* with tilting board is best, but a table of the draftsman's type, or a standard drawing board is adequate. The board should be fitted with a T-Square guide of some sort (one type is shown on page 19).

A *"floating type" two tube fluorescent lamp,* preferably of the self standing rather than the desk type, is excellent because it casts only soft shadows, and the light can be adjusted to the working area.

A *taboret,* or cabinet with drawers should be obtained for the artist's tools, paints, etc.; preferably with a compartment on the side to stack drawing paper and other material. There are many different types.

A *sturdy table* with one or more shelves for stacking material, handling large artwork, cutting and general utility use is advisable.

In addition, the artist should have the usual art tools: a drafting set (page 101), rubber cement jar and brush, cement thinner dispenser (small oil can) with thinner solution, good red sable pointed brushes, assorted pens and holders, FIG. 12, a supply of single edged razor blades, and items which are described in the sections of the book where their use is indicated.

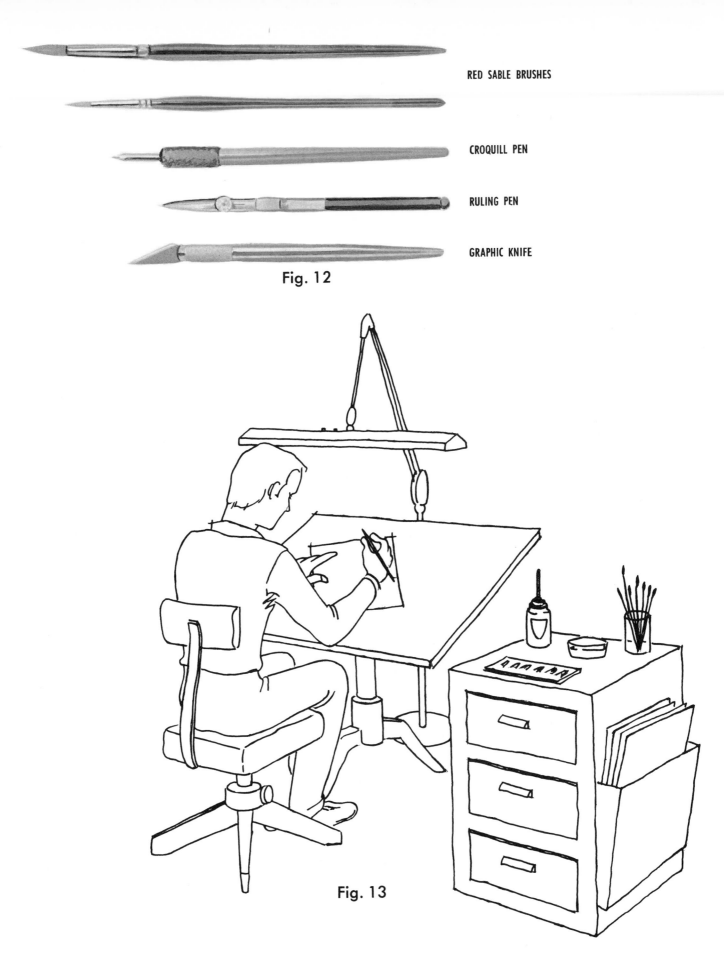

RED SABLE BRUSHES

CROQUILL PEN

RULING PEN

GRAPHIC KNIFE

Fig. 12

Fig. 13

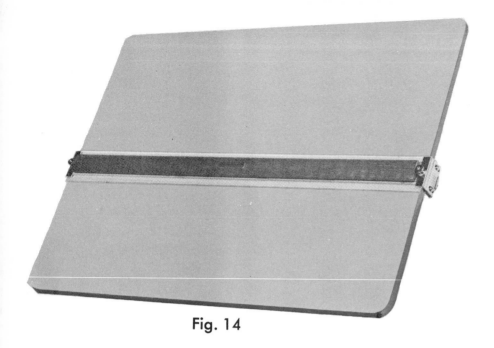

Fig. 14

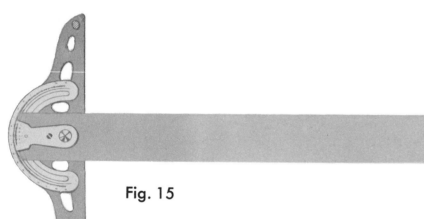

Fig. 15

Use of T-Square

FIG. 17. Since artwork for pasteups and mechanicals involves accurate measurements and alignments, all such precision work must be done with the use of a T-square and triangle. In general, the T-square is used to rule horizontal lines or parallel lines, and to guide in the pasting of horizontal copy such as type, photos, etc. The T-square is used in conjunction with a T-square guide, or "true-edge", attached to the left hand side of the board to assure proper alignment of the T-square, as any slight irregularities in the edge of the drawing board will throw the T-square out of line. The true-edge can be obtained in various lengths to fit different size boards, and it is merely clamped on as shown in FIG. 16. The true-edge can be removed easily at any time. For right-handed persons, the T-square is used with the "T" end on the left hand side so that the T-square can be shifted and held firmly with the left hand, while the right hand is being used for drawing. T-squares can be obtained made entirely of wood or of wood with plastic edges which have the advantage of enabling the artist to see the lines to which he may be adjusting the T-square as in FIG. 60, page 39. A wooden T-square will loosen up more easily than a metal one, which is firmer and more durable.

A sliding parallel, illustrated in FIG. 14, may be used in place of a T-square. This assures perfect alignment of the parallel, but has two disadvantages for the pasteup artist: (1) where the guiding cables are on the surface of the drawing board they are sometimes an obstruction: (2) the fact that the parallel cannot easily be turned at various angles other than the horizontal without making adjustments in the cables.

FIG. 15. A T-square with an adjustable head is used to rule parallel lines which are not at right angles to the edge of the drawing board. Another method of accomplishing this with an ordinary T-square is shown on page 23.

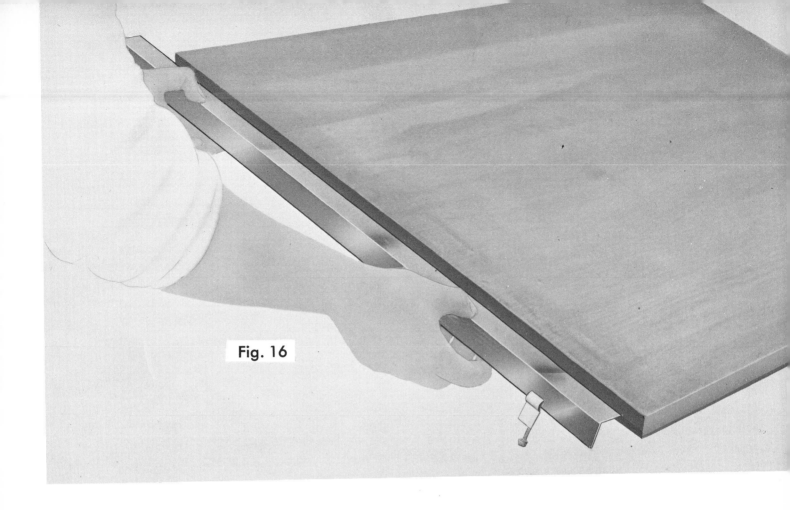

Fig. 16

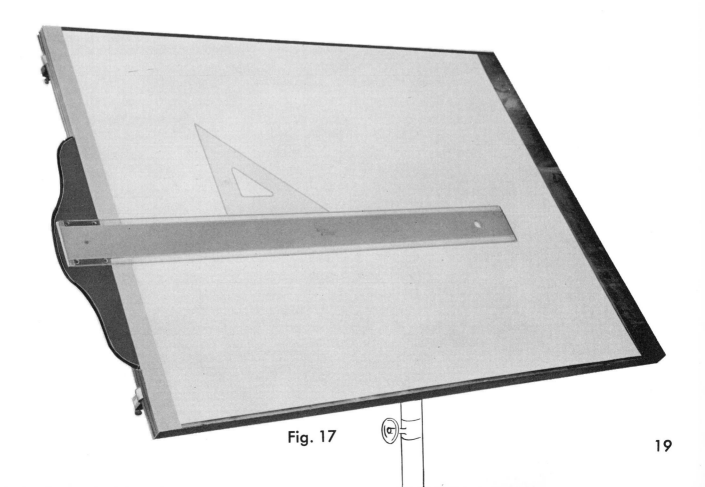

Fig. 17

19

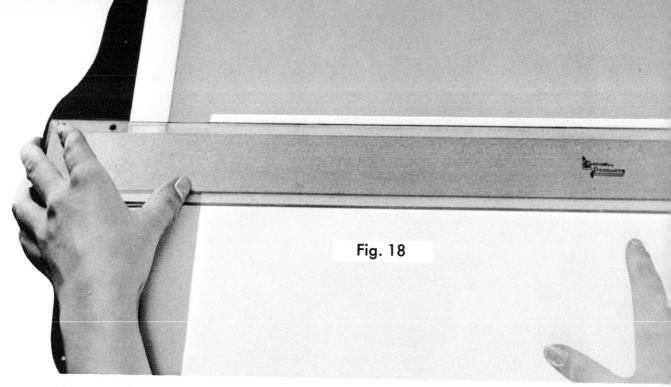

Fig. 18

Aligning the Paper

FIG. 18. In starting the pasteup or mechanical, it is necessary to line up the top edge of the paper with the T-square, so that the paper's edge is in line with the horizontal T-square when in position on the drawing board. Be sure to hold the T-square firmly against the left side of the drawing board as indicated. This should be standard practice at all times when using the T-square, as a slight change in the angle at the edge of the board will result in a considerable deviation from the true horizontal of the line being drawn.

FIG. 19. After the paper has been properly aligned, it is held down with the T-square as shown, and adhered to the drawing board with masking tape at all four corners. Masking tape has the following advantages over thumb tacks: holes are not put into the drawing board, the paper does not loosen as easily, and the T-square and triangle will slide more easily over the flat tape.

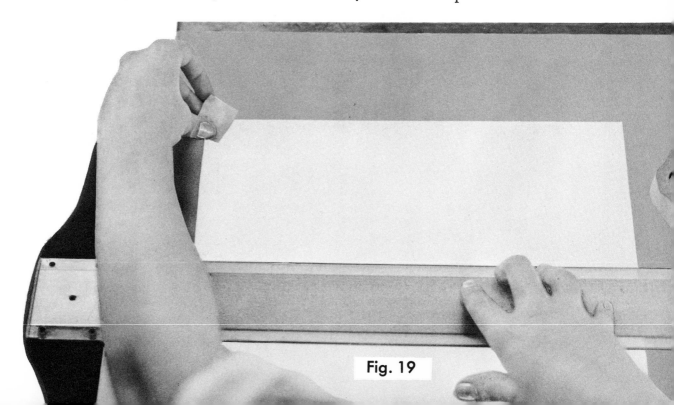

Fig. 19

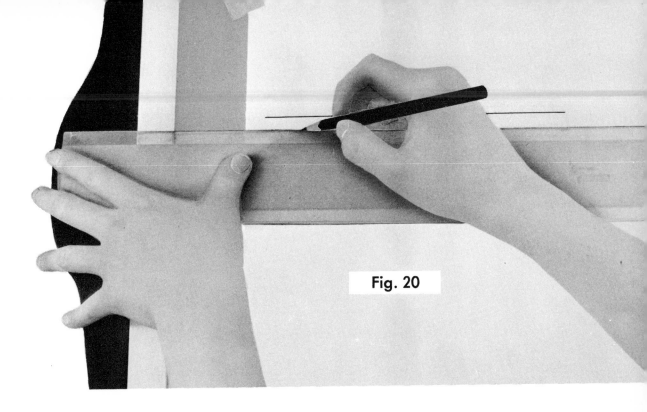

Fig. 20

FIG. 20. Since the top of the paper has been aligned with the T-square held in a horizontal position, any line now drawn with the T-square will be horizontal and parallel to the top edge of the paper. To draw successive parallel lines one merely shifts the T-square to the proper position and draws the line with the pencil held firmly against the edge of the T-square. Do not shift the angle of the pencil while drawing the line, as this will produce an irregular line.

FIG. 21. To draw, with the T-square, lines parallel to each other but not parallel to the top edge of the paper, shift the paper to the proper angle, as shown, then rule the lines as usual, with the T-square. The paper can be shifted to any angle for this purpose.

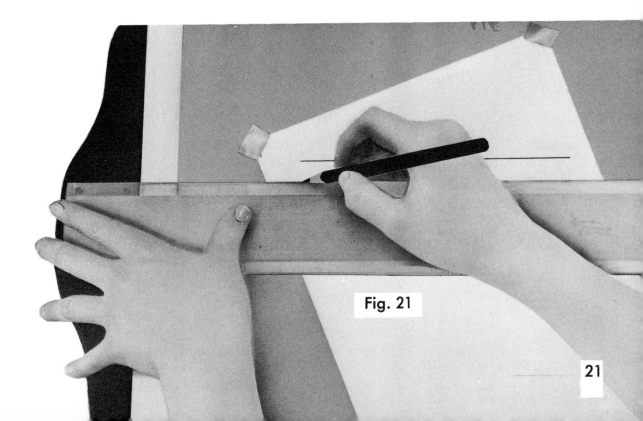

Fig. 21

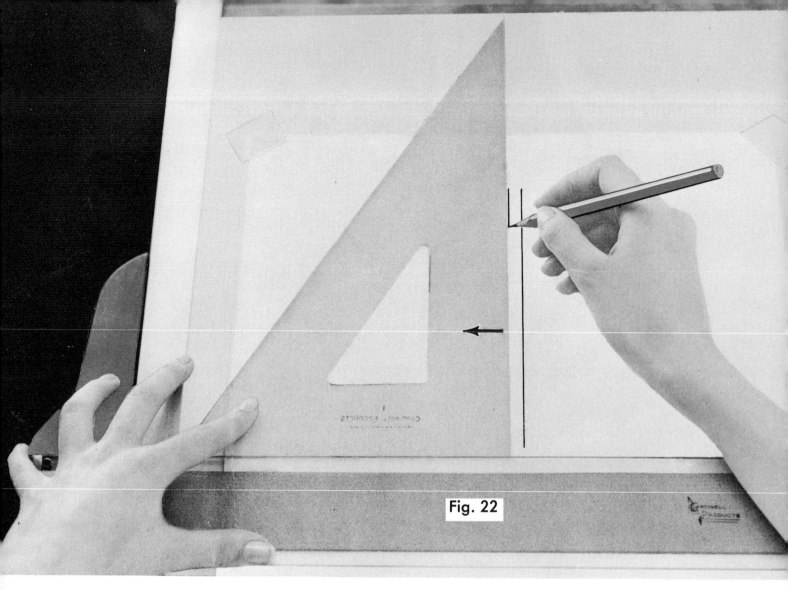

Fig. 22

Use of Triangle

FIG. 22. Vertical lines are drawn with a right-angle triangle held firmly against the T-square, which is properly held against the side of the board. Successive parallel lines can be drawn merely by shifting the triangle as indicated by the arrow. Do not attempt to draw accurate vertical lines by shifting the T-square from the side to the top of the drawing board, as the horizontals and verticals will not be at right angles unless the board itself is perfectly square, which is rarely the case.

If a vertical line to be drawn is longer than the triangle being used, the T-square is merely lowered after the line is partly drawn, the triangle placed in position against the line already drawn, and the line extended. Another method of extending the line would be to draw it the length of the triangle, then place the edge of the T-square, or a long rule, along the line and extend it to whatever length is necessary.

FIG. 23. Lines can be drawn at any angle by using an adjustable triangle. This has a movable side which can be regulated to any degree desired by means of a protractor.

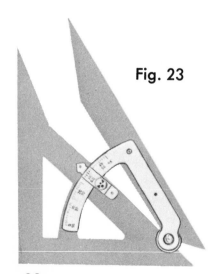

Fig. 23

The following procedure can also be used to draw lines parallel to a previous line which is not parallel to the top or side edges of the paper; FIG. 24. A triangle is brought up to the line. FIG. 25. The edge of the T-square is carefully brought up to the triangle. FIG. 26. By sliding the triangle along the edge of the T-square, lines parallel to the first one can be drawn at any distance from the original line. Do not allow the T-square to shift during this operation.

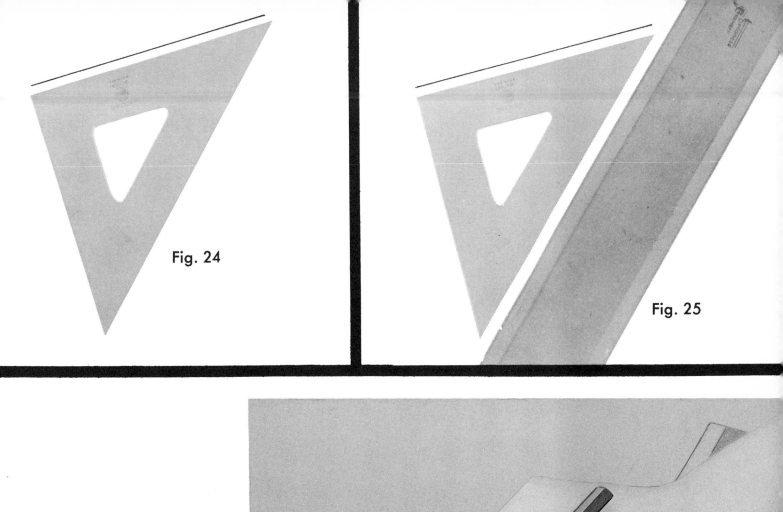

Fig. 24

Fig. 25

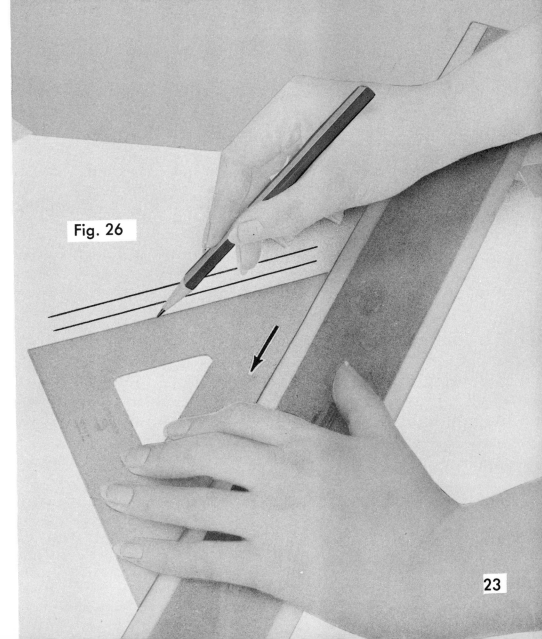

Fig. 26

CUTTING AND TRIMMING

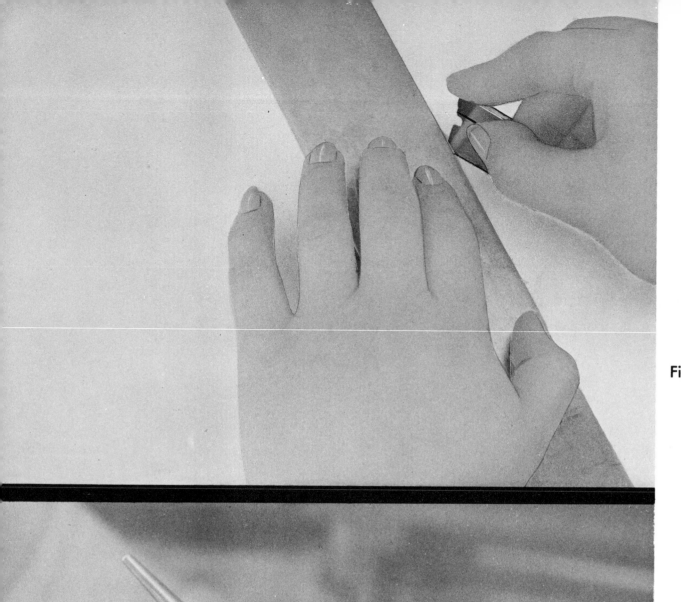

Fig. 27

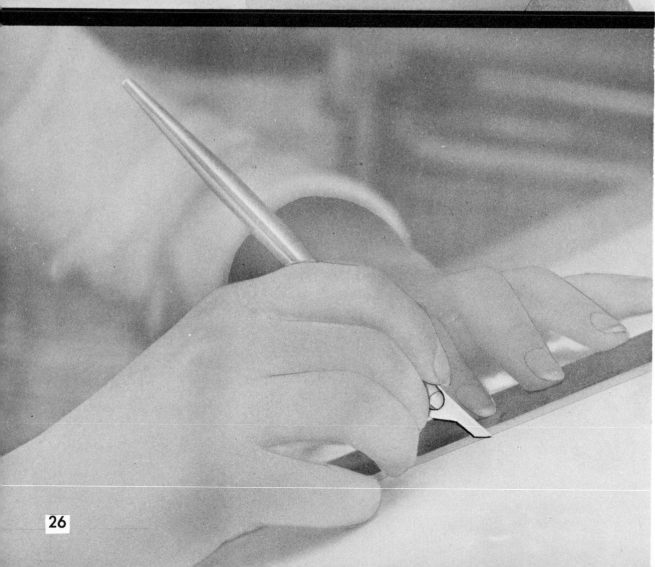

Fig. 28

Cutting

Accurate cutting is involved in pasteup work because reproduction proofs, photostats, photographs, mounting board, drawing paper, and illustration board often have to be trimmed to size. In some instances a paper cutter is practical; but, for the most part, the pasteup artist works with a metal straight edge or rule, and single edge razor blade, or mat knife, FIGS. 27, 28 and 29. Cutting is best done with the point of the razor blade or knife held firmly against the metal edge. There should be no lateral sway of the knife or straight edge when cutting, as this will result in an irregular line. More pressure should be exerted on the straight edge than on the knife as most irregular cutting is caused by the shifting of the former. Cutting is best done on a hard surface such as glass or metal, as a clean cut edge results, though it wears down the blade more quickly. See page 28 for instructions on sharpening blades.

Cutting through illustration board or mat board is best done by cutting over the same line several times. Again, be sure to hold the blade at the same angle each time so that the line will not be ragged.

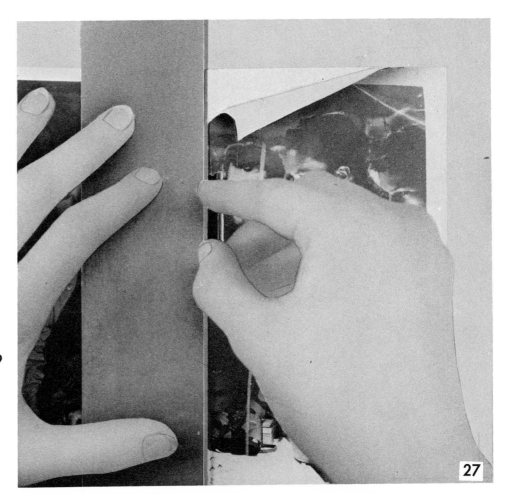

Fig. 29

Sharpening Knives and Blades

To retain a good cutting edge, blades must be sharpened periodically, since they are easily dulled when cutting paper. This can be done on an oil stone or a fine carborundum stone. A drop or two of pike oil may be used to lubricate the stone. The blade should be held, FIGS. 30 and 31, at such angle to the stone that the beveled cutting edge lies flat on the stone.

FIG. 32 is an enlarged diagram which shows this more clearly. While the blade is held firmly in this position, it is moved back and forth in a straight line parallel to the long edge of the stone, then turned over, and the other side of the bevel sharpened. Be certain to retain the same angle of bevel on each side. After sharpening, remove any remaining burrs by passing the blade lightly over a smooth Arkansas stone.

FIG. 33. Various types of blades and knives for studio use are illustrated. A—A pointed knife, good for clean accurate cutting. B—A curved blade for cutting, and also useful for scraping ink off of acetate overlays when corrections are necessary. C—A swivel blade knife, useful for cutting curves. D—A heavy mat knife for cutting mats and cardboard.

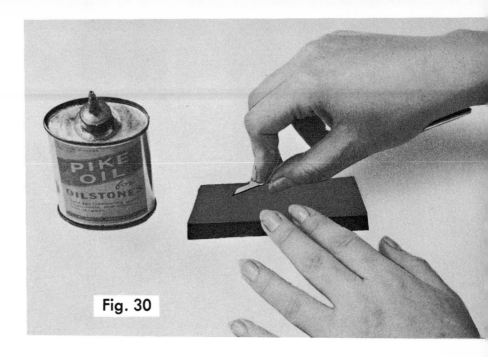

Fig. 30

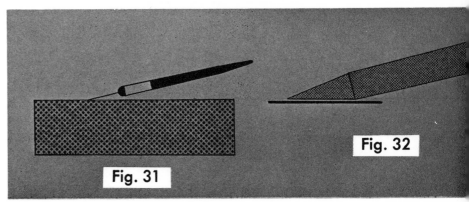

Fig. 31

Fig. 32

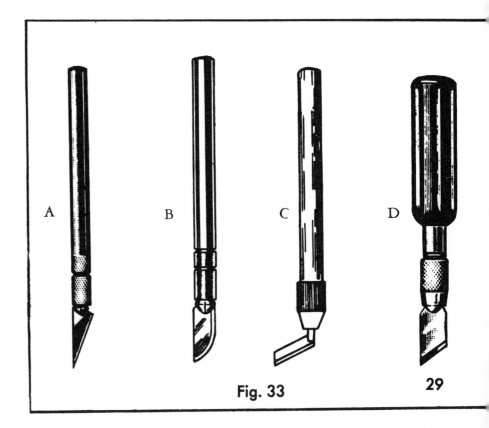

A   B   C   D

Fig. 33

29

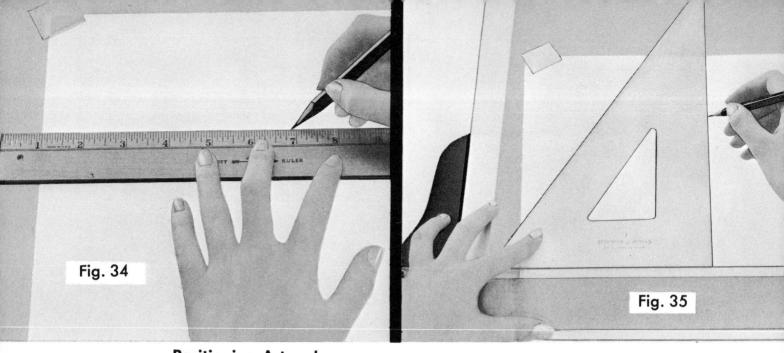

Fig. 34

Fig. 35

Positioning Artwork

Pasteups and mechanicals involve positioning of artwork within a specific area of specific size, usually a rectangular one. When a square or rectangle of specific dimension is to be drawn and centered on a sheet of paper, the following procedure is best used:

FIG. 34. Obtain the *vertical* center of the sheet of paper by measuring off the width of the paper and halving it. Note that the measurement is made from the 1 inch mark on this ruler rather than from the actual end of the ruler. A more accurate measurement can be obtained by this method as the ruler may be worn slightly where the measurements start at the edge.

FIG. 35. Through this center draw a vertical line from top to bottom of the sheet, using the T-square and triangle.

FIG. 36. Obtain the *horizontal* center of the paper by measuring it and halving it and,

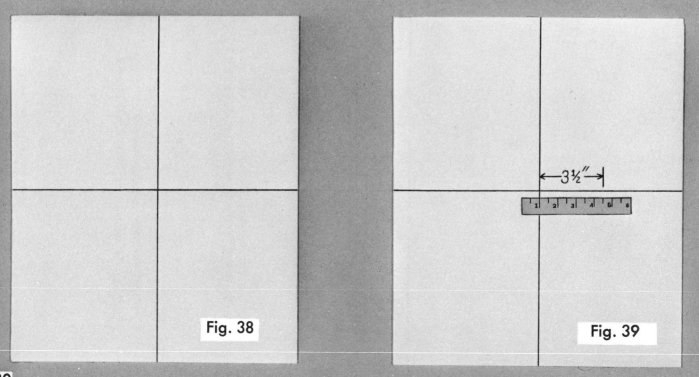

Fig. 38

Fig. 39

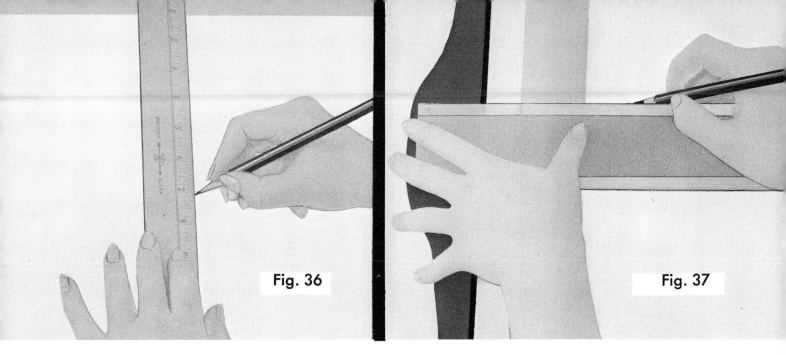

Fig. 36

Fig. 37

FIG. 37. draw a horizontal line with the T-square through this point.

FIG. 38. The sheet of paper is shown with the vertical and horizontal center lines drawn.

FIG. 39. If the rectangle required is 7 inches wide, measure off 3½ inches on either side of the vertical center line and draw verticals through these points with the T-square and triangle.

FIG. 40. If the vertical dimension is 8 inches, measure off 4 inches, above and below the horizontal center line, and

FIG. 41 draw horizontal lines through these points with the T-square. We now have a rectangle of proper size centered on the paper. It can readily be seen that the same basic procedure may be followed for placing any size rectangle or square in any other area of the sheet, or in any specific location within this rectangle, which might represent the dimensions of a page or an ad.

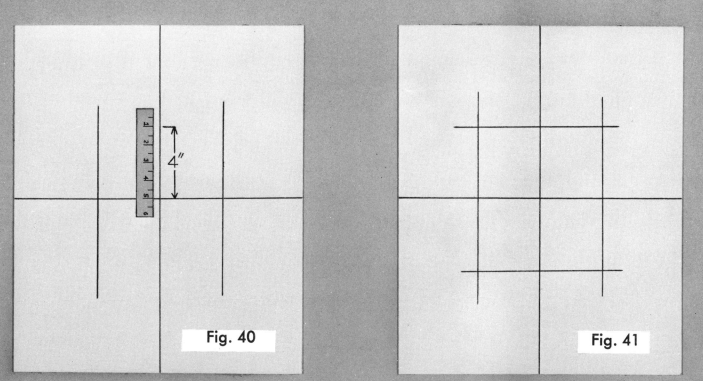

Fig. 40

Fig. 41

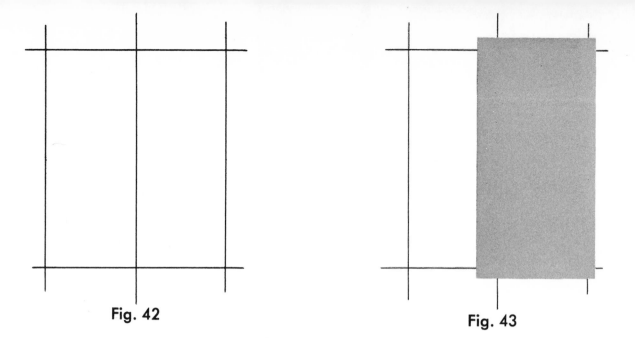

Fig. 42

Fig. 43

Cutting Flush Edges (Mortising)

Often it is necessary to flush-mount two photographs, pieces of paper, or artwork so that there is no overlap or space between them. This is best accomplished by the following procedure:

FIG. 42. Suppose we have to trim and mount equal size sheets of light and dark gray paper in a rectangular area, with no overlap or space between the two. All outside edges are to be trimmed flush to the rectangle. Note in this illustration that all dimension lines have been extended beyond the corners and center of the rectangle proper. The purpose of this will be indicated in FIG. 45.

FIG. 43. Using the dry mount rubber cement method, page 37, lay down the light gray paper. It has been cut to a size slightly larger than the rectangular area it is to cover, so that it overlaps the center line as well as the outside edges of the rectangle.

FIG. 44. Now lay down the dark gray paper in the other half of the rectangle so that it slightly overlaps both the center line and the light gray paper.

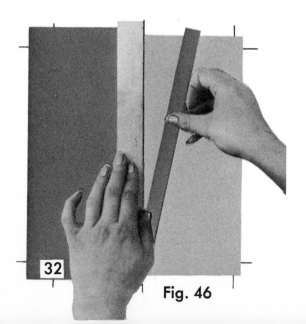

Fig. 46

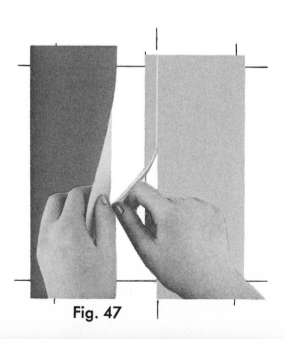

Fig. 47

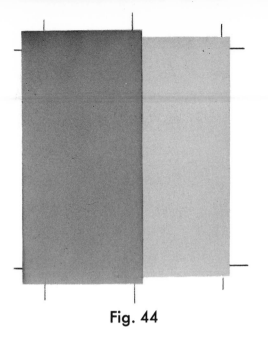

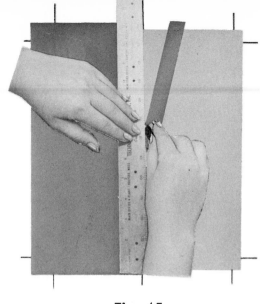

Fig. 44   **Fig. 45**

FIG. 45. Using a metal straight-edge on the center line, cut sharply through both pieces of paper at the same time with a razor blade.

FIG. 46. Remove the overlapping strip of dark gray paper just cut off.

FIG. 47. With the left hand, carefully lift the dark gray paper along the center line, and remove the overlapping strip of light gray paper which has remained underneath it.

FIG. 48. Drop the edge of the dark gray paper back into position along the center and, using a sheet of tracing paper to protect the gray paper, rub both edges down where they meet.

FIG. 49. With a straight-edge lined up horizontally across the top, trim both light and dark gray papers at one time, using the corner trim lines as a guide. This method assures much more accuracy than could possibly be obtained by cutting both pieces of paper individually and placing them in position. The trim marks can be erased if necessary.

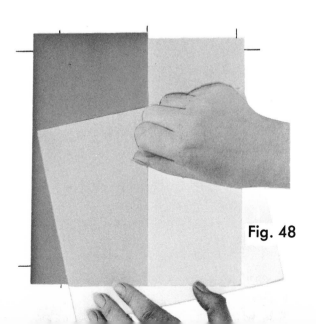

Fig. 48

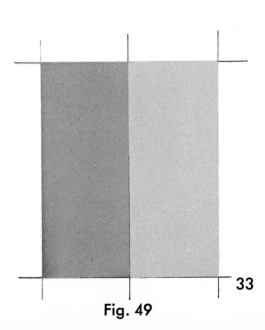

33

Fig. 49

PASTING UP

Use of Rubber Cement

Rubber cement is used for pasting and mounting photographs, type proofs and artwork, because it does not stain paper, and can be readily be removed from the surface after it has dried. Rubber cement is obtainable in jars or cans, and should be purchased in pint or larger sizes for general pasteup work. It is then transferred to a rubber cement dispenser. A rubber cement solvent is obtainable for thinning the cement when it thickens in the jar, from exposure to air or infrequent use.

Two general types of dispensers are in use:

FIG. 50. The glass dispenser with an adjustable brush in the cap allows the brush to be adjusted to the level of cement in the jar, so that the brush will not dry out, yet avoid having the handle submerged completely in rubber cement. The jar is usually amber colored to ward off light rays which can affect the rubber cement. Rubber cement dispensers of this type are obtainable in pint and quart sizes.

FIG. 51. A rubber cement dispenser for use on large areas is obtainable in the form of a can with a cone-shaped top. The brush remains in the can and its handle fits into the cone-shaped top. The can contains a wire bracket against which the flat brush can be rubbed before use, to remove excess rubber cement.

FIG. 52. When applying rubber cement to a surface, the excess cement should be removed against the inside edge of the jar and the cement applied to the paper with even, horizontal, overlapping strokes, just as one would apply a wash of color. It is not necessary to adhere strictly within the limits of the area to be covered, as the excess rubber cement can be removed. For *permanent* mounting, both the mounting surface and the back of the artwork or photograph to be mounted are covered with rubber cement and allowed to dry completely (a minute or two) before being placed in contact with each other. This shall be referred to as "dry" mounting. Since the rubber cement will adhere immediately under such conditions, precautions in mounting should be followed as indicated on page 80. For

Fig. 50

Fig. 51

36

temporary mounting, the back of a photograph or artwork is covered with rubber cement, and it is placed on the uncoated mounting board immediately while it is wet.

FIG. 53. After any excess rubber cement surrounding the artwork has dried, it may be removed by using a rubber cement pickup, FIG. 54, or a piece of masking tape, FIG. 55. A rubber cement pickup may be made by slopping rubber cement on the outside of the glass jar, allowing it to dry, then rolling it into a ball. Masking tape is used by folding a small piece of tape back on itself, adhesive side out, so that the two ends adhere to each other. The adhesive surface of the tape or the pickup, when placed in contact with rubber cement, removes the rubber cement, either by rubbing or by dabbing—the latter when there is a possibility of scratching the surface of the paper or artwork.

Fig. 52

Fig. 53

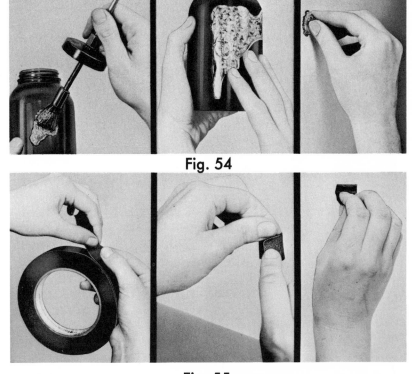

Fig. 54

Fig. 55

Proofs from NEWARK NEWS

WHEEL YOUR OWN DEAL
BOSS MOTORS
SALE!
BOSS

Fig. 56

Pasteup Procedure

Captions and text material, carefully printed on coated paper stock, from hand set or machine set type, are known as reproduction proofs. The simplest form of pasteup involves the assemblage of such material according to a given layout.

FIG. 56. To indicate the basic procedure involved let us select one line from a repro proof which has several captions on it, and paste this one line in position on another sheet of paper. Let us assume that "WHEEL YOUR OWN DEAL" is required for a given layout.

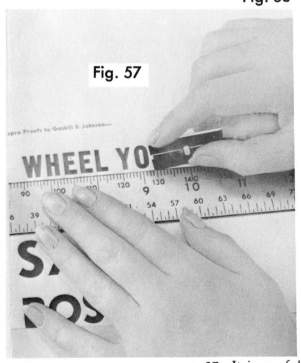

Fig. 57

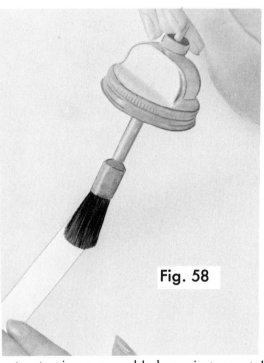

Fig. 58

FIG. 57. It is carefully cut out using a razor blade against a metal straight edge, leaving at least a sixteenth of an inch margin around the lettering. Be certain to hold the ruler down firmly while cutting. Avoid rubbing the hand or ruler over the type, to prevent smearing and soiling. The type may be sprayed with a clear fixatif to help avoid smearing during pasteup. Fixatif is available in spray cans.

FIG. 58. Place the type proof face down on a clean surface, dab each end with rubber cement and, while wet, place in position.

FIG. 59. This may be done either with the fingers, the fingers and a razor blade, or, if the pieces are small, with a pair of tweezers. While the rubber cement is wet, the proof may be shifted so that the base of the letters is properly aligned with a previously drawn pencil guide line, or, FIG. 60, it may be lined up with a T-square. When in its proper position it can be smoothed down by rubbing on a piece of clean paper placed over the type. Any excess rubber cement can be cleaned off the mount or proof with a pick-up *after it is dry.* If done while the excess rubber cement is wet the type may smear.

Fig. 59

Larger reproduction proofs may be coated around the entire edge with cement instead of merely dabbed at each corner. Sometimes proofs are dry mounted, but in such cases extreme care has to be taken when placing the proofs in position as they cannot be shifted once contact with the mounting surface has been made. If necessary, the proof can be removed with rubber cement thinner as shown on page 75. Certain typographers now supply type proofs with an adhesive coating on the back so they can be adhered merely by rubbing down.

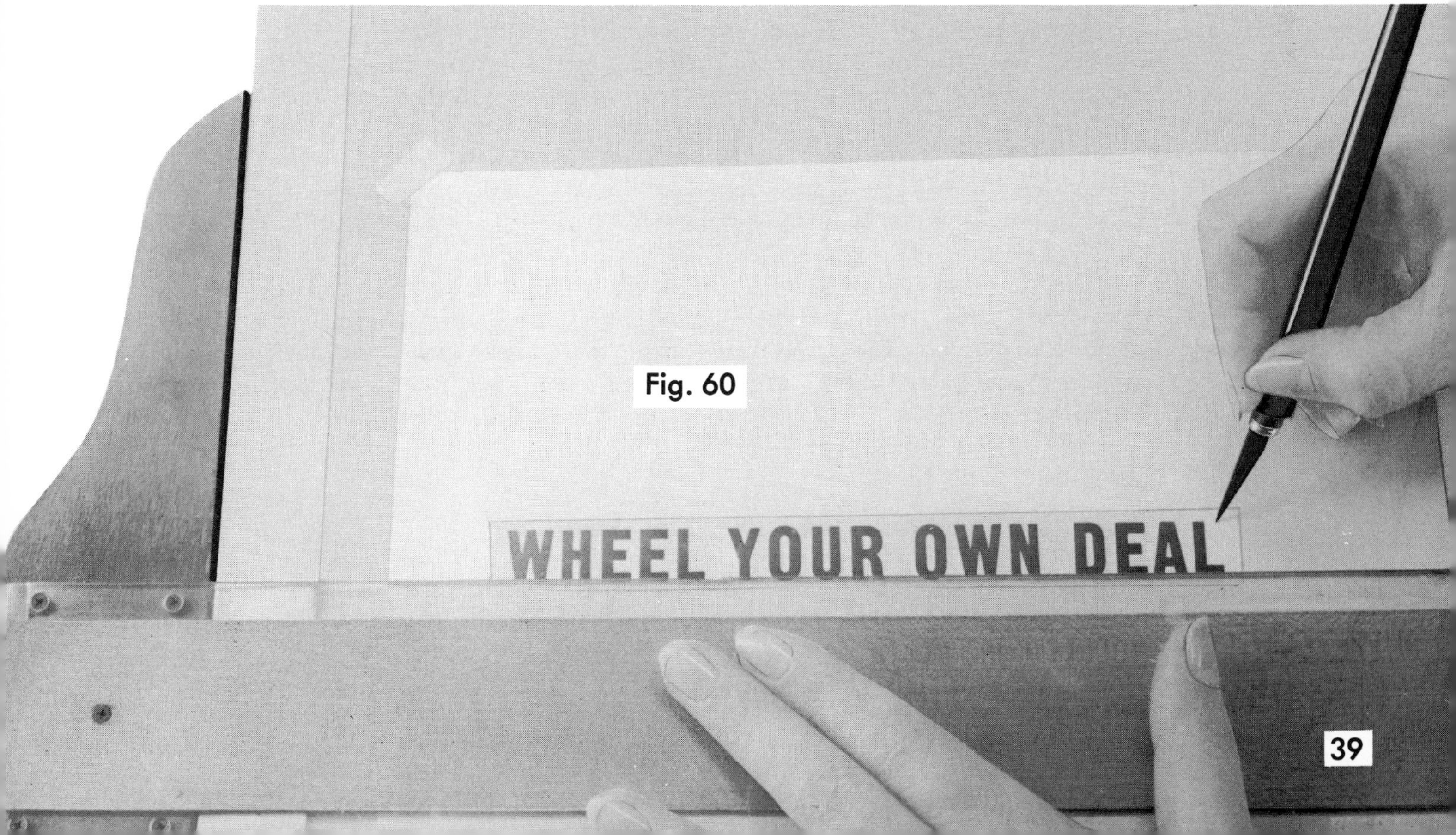

Fig. 60

Pasting Up Type

In this example, we have a reproduction proof of several paragraphs of copy, printed in position, in addition to a negative photostat of an illustration, and two strips of single line captions. It is necessary to paste this up as a mechanical and enclose the body copy with a thin pen line border. Let us consider only this last operation. Since the actual size of the area to be enclosed by a border has been predetermined by the layout artist, and the reproduction proof prepared to allow adequate margin on all sides, the border is inked in first with a ruling pen, using the T-square and triangle (see page 102). The reproduction proof is cut out, care being taken not to cut too close to the lettering, but close enough so that the proof is not larger than the inked border. This proof is *wet mounted;* that is, rubber cement applied only to the back of the proof, not to the illustration board; and the proof placed in position quickly, while the rubber cement is still wet and fairly thick.

FIG. 61. In order to assure speed and accuracy before mounting, the centers of the top and bottom border lines were marked with a blue pencil, as were the centers of the top and bottom of the proof, thus the proof could be immediately centered vertically by registering these four marks. (Refer to page 30.) These blue marks would not actually show in reproduction, but are allowed to reproduce here for clarity. Note also that when placing the proof in position the sides of the proof are curved upwards so that only the center comes in contact with the board at first, then the two edges are allowed to drop down.

FIG. 62. The top line of type is now lined up with the T-square. (See detail, FIG. 63.) Since the rubber cement is still wet, the proof can be maneuvered into exact position if not already there. After being placed in position, the proof is covered with a sheet of tracing paper for protection and pressed firmly to the illustration board. When using this method, either the entire back of the proof can be coated with rubber cement, or a quarter inch area along the back edges so coated, or just a dab of rubber cement may be placed in each corner.

If the block of copy is set with the understanding that a border is to be drawn around it *after* the particular size of the block of copy is determined, the reproduction proof could be placed in position first, the excess paper of the proof cut off on all sides, and then the border drawn with the ruling pen, T-square, and triangle, after first positioning the lines in blue pencil.

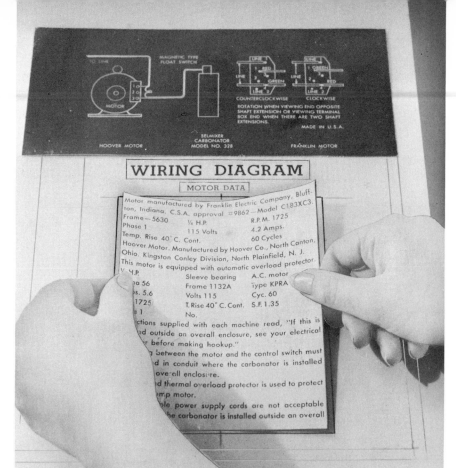

Fig. 61

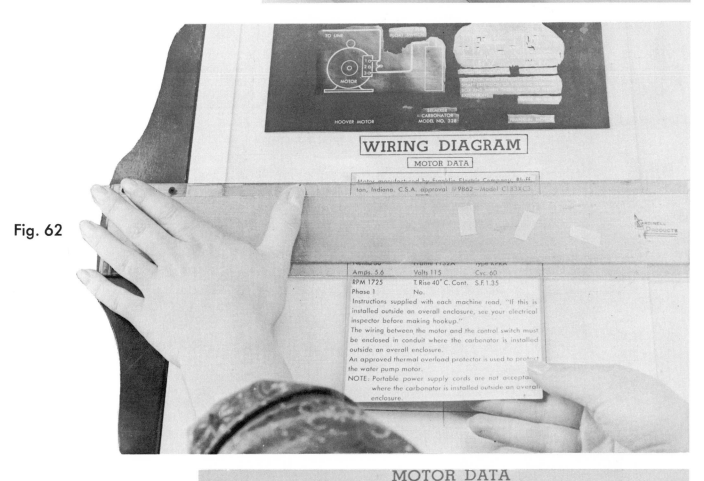

Fig. 62

Fig. 63

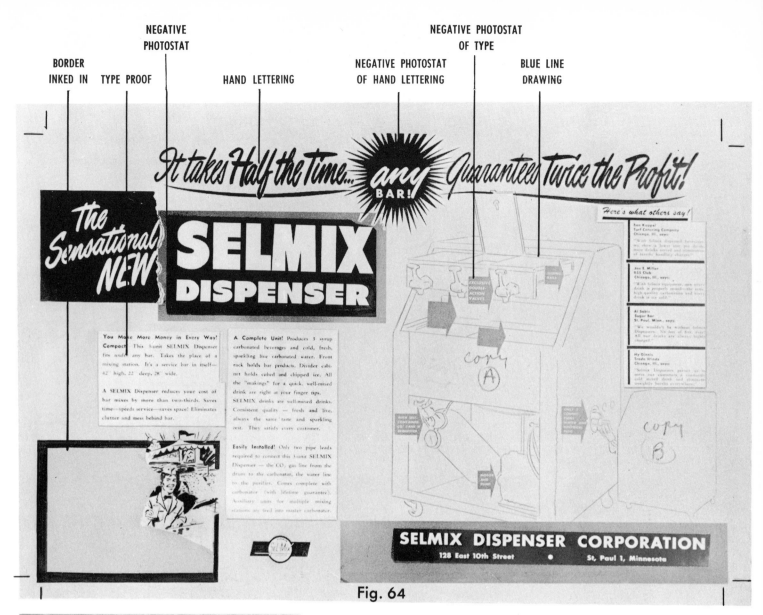

Fig. 64

Fig. 65

Combining Type, Photos, Art and Stats

FIG. 64. This mechanical consists of various components: 1. Hand lettering in ink, directly on the mechanical; 2. A negative photostat of hand lettering; 3. Hand lettering in poster white on black ink background; 4. Negative photostat of printed type (repro proof); 5. Pen and ink drawing directly on the mechanical; 6. Blue outline drawing to show position of photographs to be inserted (stripped in) in the platemaking state; 7. Type (repro proofs of body copy) pasted in position.

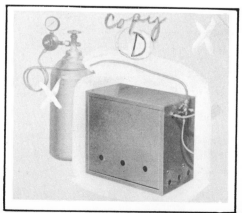

Fig. 66

42

Fig. 67

This comparatively complicated assemblage of art is a good example of the method of handling varied units. Naturally, the pasteup artist would not be expected to do the spot drawing, or even the hand lettering, unless he were trained in these arts. Of particular interest is the manner in which the photographs are handled. First of all, they are too large to be pasted directly in position on the mechanical; and secondly, this promotion piece is to be printed once with one set of photographs, indicated in FIG. 64, then with another set, shown in FIG. 67; and thirdly, it is not advisable to combine halftone art (the photos) directly with line art in a mechanical. The position of the photos is indicated by means of a blue pencil or blue ink outline, which drops out when photographed, but serves as a guide for the engraver. The outline was allowed to reproduce in this illustration for instruction purposes. One outline contains the note "copy A" and the other "copy B", which corresponds to similar notes on the respective photographs to go into these positions. For the second set of photographs to be printed on the alternate version of this promotion piece, we mark "copy C" and "copy D" as shown in FIGS. 65 and 66. The position of these photos on the mechanical would be shown on an overlay which would replace the outlines now indicated. See page 48 for the methods of scaling photographs. FIG. 67. The reproduction of the promotion piece as it would actually appear, with photos C and D in position.

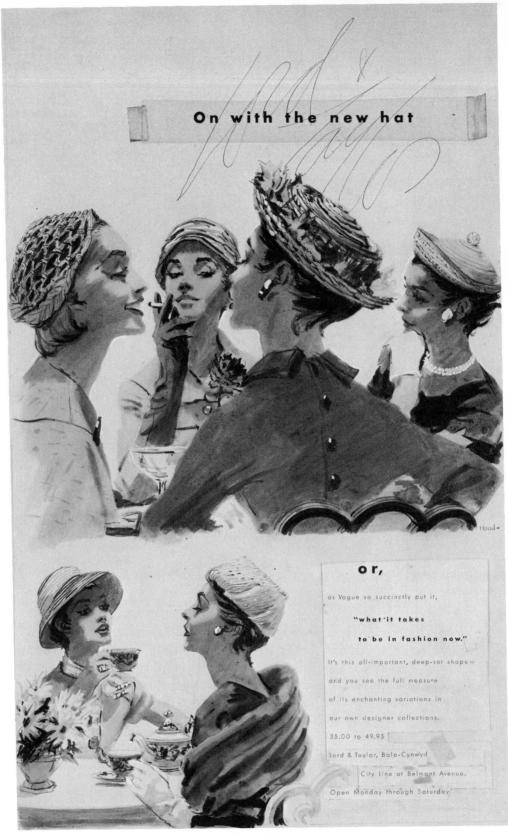

Fig. 68

Stripping-In Lettering

A simple pasteup prepared for newspaper advertising is shown on this page, and the reproduction, as it appeared in the newspaper, is shown on the next page. The heading, which consists of a combination of a line of type superimposed over hand lettering, was prepared by printing the type proof on transparent acetate, and placing this, on the original art, over the hand lettering. (This could also have been handled by printing the type proof on paper

On with the new hat

or,

as Vogue so succinctly put it,

"what it takes

to be in fashion now."

It's this all-important, deep-set shape—

and you see the full measure

of its enchanting variations in

our own designer collections.

35.00 to 49.95

Lord & Taylor, Bala-Cynwyd

City Line at Belmont Avenue.

Open Monday through Saturday

Fig. 69

as usual; then, indicating its position as an overlay on the hand lettering, instruct the engraver to strip it in.) The proof of the body copy is shown pasted in position in the lower right portion of the ad.

The left hand illustration is printed in this book with a fine screen so that details, pasteup marks and tonal values show well for instruction purposes. The right hand page is reproduced in coarse screen, 65 line, as it actually was in the newspaper.

SCALING AND CROPPING

Fig. 70

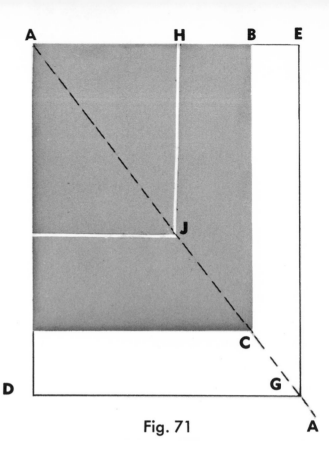

Fig. 71

Scaling

Photographs and artwork may exist, or be prepared, in sizes other than those at which they will eventually be reproduced. This may involve reduction or enlargement of the entire image to the necessary size. While this will be done photographically, when the material is copied for plate making, it is necessary to determine in advance exactly what proportion and area the art work or photograph will assume when enlarged or reduced, and to properly indicate this on the artwork, for the platemaker's information. This is known as scaling. Such a situation occurred in the mechanical shown on page 42. You might ask why the photographs are not made the correct size in the first place by the photographer. Commercial photographs are generally made in standard sizes, as explained in a later section of this book, and submitted to the editors, the advertising agencies, the firms or persons who may or not have ordered the photographs. Consider the particular one used here, which is a publicity photograph of an actress, publicizing a movie, sent to numerous newspapers, magazines and public relations organizations, who may possibly reproduce it, and in various unpredictable sizes. Since it has to be copied for the plate-making phase of reproduction, it will be enlarged or reduced during this process to the desired size. In this case, though altered in size, the entire image is used. It is common practice to select and use only a *portion* of the image, as shown on pages 58 and 59. This is known as *cropping,* and will be considered separately so as not to be confusing.

Consider, for example, the photograph in FIG. 70. It is possible to reduce this to the size and proportion represented by FIG. 72, or enlarge it to that represented by FIG. 73. Note that in each case exactly the same image area is included. Any photograph or piece of artwork can be scaled by the following procedure:

Fig. 72

Fig. 73

FIG. 71. Assume that the gray rectangular area represents the photograph shown on the left. A diagonal line, dotted line AA, is drawn through the photograph. If it is desired to enlarge the photograph to the width AE (2¾″) the top line of the photograph is extended to this point. To determine what the proportionate new *depth* of the photograph will be with this extended width, a vertical is dropped from E till it meets the diagonal, which will occur at Point G. The line EG now represents the new depth of the photograph, and when measured is found to be 3¾″. Thus, if the original photograph, 2¼″ wide and 3″ deep is enlarged to a width of 2¾″ the new proportionate depth will be 3¾″.

If the controlling measurement is the new *depth* of the photograph, rather than the width, the side, instead of the top, would be extended to the new size AD. Then from point D a horizontal is extended to the diagonal, giving the new width of DG.

The same procedure may be used to obtain the reduction of a photograph. Assume that we wish to reduce the photograph to the new width AH. The vertical is dropped from this point to the same diagonal, and the distance HJ represents the new depth at this reduction.

While this procedure may seem somewhat complicated, repetition of the process will make it clearer and easier to perform. On the following pages, for further clarification the procedure is shown step-by-step as it would actually be performed on photographs.

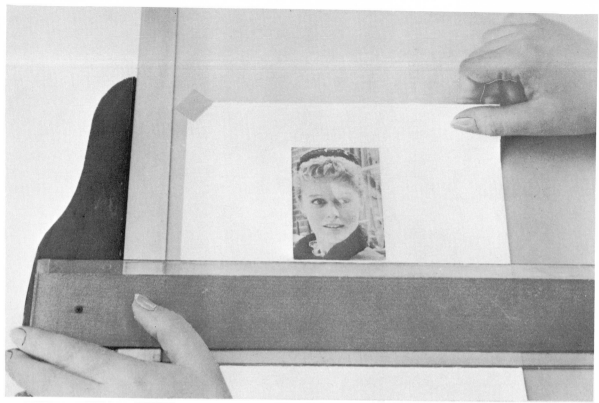

Fig. 74

Scaling a Photo (Enlarging)

FIG. 74. Line up the top or bottom of the photo image with the T-square and secure the photo in place with masking tape. This image we are working with measures 2¼″ wide by 3″ deep. We wish to enlarge it to a width of 2¾″ and determine its depth at this enlarged size.

FIG. 75. Draw a diagonal from the top left corner through the bottom right corner, extending it a short distance beyond. Be certain to draw the line accurately through each corner. (The diagonal might just as well have been drawn from top right to bottom left, in which case the procedure of scaling would be the same, but it would be a reversal or mirror image of the procedure now followed.) A grease pencil, lithographic pencil or china marking pencil is used on the photograph proper, as such markings can be removed easily (page 66) from photographs, but not from the artwork or tracing paper.

FIG. 76. From the top left corner measure 2¾″ across the top of the photo, to the right, extending a line to this point.

FIG. 77. At this point, using the T-square and triangle, drop a vertical until it reaches the diagonal. If the diagonal you have drawn is too short merely extend it sufficiently.

FIG. 78. A line drawn from this point across to the left side of the photo marks off the area of the new enlargement.

FIG. 79. Measuring the new vertical dimension of the photo gives 3¾″. So the original 2¼″ x 3″ photo has been scaled to enlarge to 2¾″ x 3¾″.

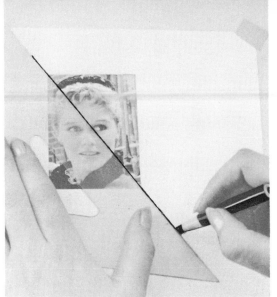

Fig. 75

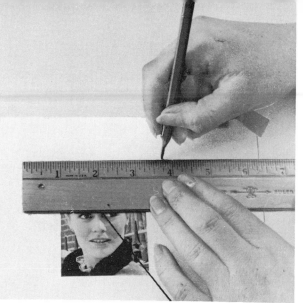

Fig. 76

Fig. 77

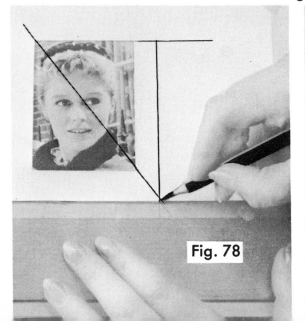

Fig. 78

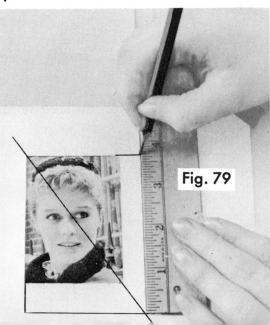

Fig. 79

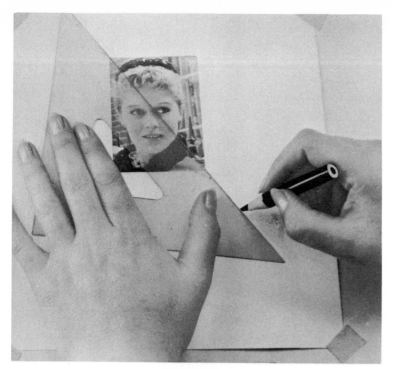

Fig. 80

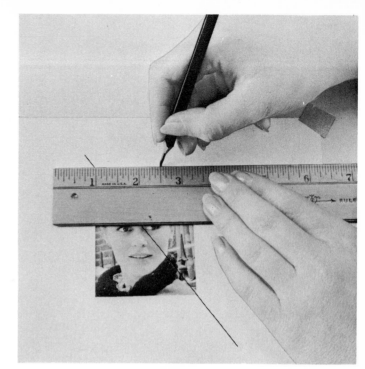

Fig. 81

Scaling a Photo (Reducing)

To scale a photo for reduction the same basic process is used.

FIG. 80. Draw a diagonal through the photo as before.

FIG. 81. Measure off the new desired width at the top, 1½″.

FIG. 82. Drop a vertical from this to the diagonal. Instead of being on the outside of the photo, as previously when enlarging, this line is now on the inside, because the new size is smaller.

FIG. 83. Extend the width from this point to the left.

FIG. 84. Measure off the new vertical, which is 2″. The new reduced photo will measure 1½″ x 2″.

FIG. 85. The photo in its reduced reproduction.

Fig. 82

Fig. 83

Fig. 84

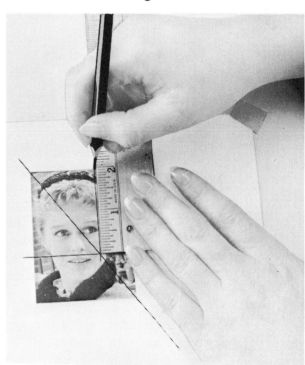

Fig. 85

Fig. 86

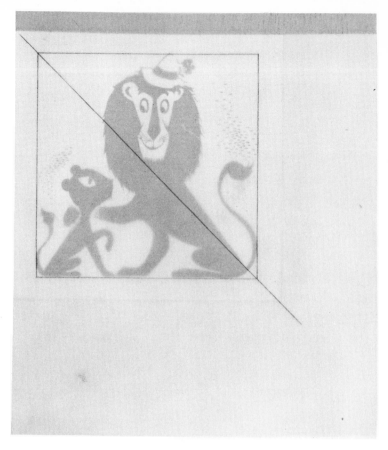

Fig. 87

Scaling (Irregular Shapes)

Not all artwork or photographs have a square or rectangular shape, insofar as the image is concerned. FIG. 86. This drawing is a case in point. Artwork or a photograph of this nature, that is, an irregularly shaped image against a white, undefined background, is known as a "silhouette", in printing terms.

FIG. 87. To scale this for enlargement or reduction place a sheet of tracing paper over it, adhering it across the top with masking tape. Box in the drawing at its extreme dimensions at the top, bottom and both sides, using a T-square and triangle. You can now draw the usual diagonal and proceed with scaling as in previous examples. Dimension guides and size can be put on the overlay and the artwork sent to the platemaker in this manner. The overlay will be lifted or removed for photo copying of the original art. If it is necessary to indicate the crop marks and dimension on the original art this can be done in blue pencil if the original is *line* art only, and if halftone art, it can be done as in FIG. 112, page 67, which also shows how to convert a photograph with a background into a silhouette photo.

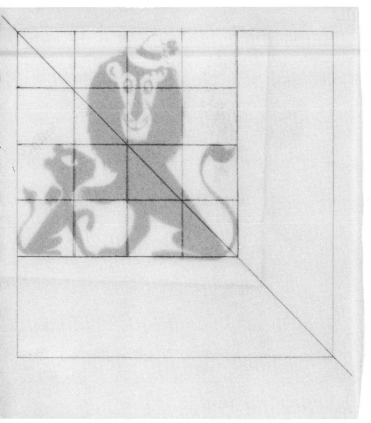

Fig. 88   Fig. 89

If it is necessary to determine what the actual image will look like in the new size, or if necessary to scale a sketch to a new size to make a finished drawing, several methods can be used. The least time consuming for the artist would be to have a photostat made of the drawing to the new size, then trace it and transfer it. If no such service is readily available, or the additional expense a factor, the "square-up" method is practical:

FIG. 88. Starting with the step shown in the previous illustration, extend the top or side to the new size desired and complete the rectangle. Divide the small rectangle boxing the drawing, into quarter sections, forming a grid of lines over the drawing.

FIG. 89. Redraw the large rectangle on the paper you wish the enlargement to appear on, and divide this into quarter sections, which will be correspondingly enlarged sections of the small grid. Using these grids as guides, redraw the image in its new size.

Other methods of enlarging or reducing images visually for drawing are by the use of a pantograph and the camera lucida, as explained on the next page.

Fig. 90

Fig. 91

Fig. 92

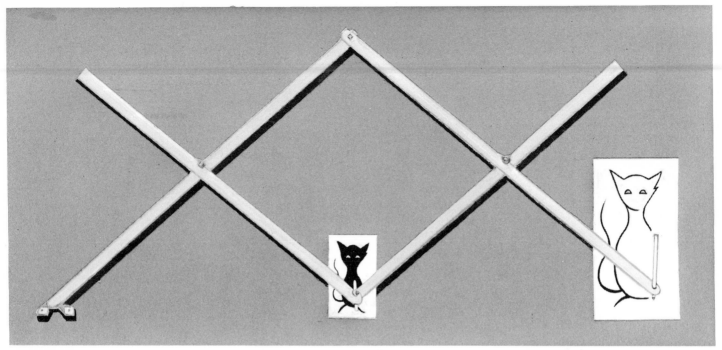

Fig. 93

Tracing and Scaling Devices

FIG. 90. Most tracing paper is semi-opaque, which results in the loss of a certain amount of detail when placed over a delicate drawing or photograph with subtle tones. To overcome this handicap, a lightbox can be used. This is a glass-topped box with lights inside, FIG. 91, which can be purchased in art supply stores or easily made.

FIG. 92. In use, the lights are turned on, the photo placed on the glass top, and the tracing paper placed over it. Both are taped in position. Note how much clearer the image is, as compared with the previous one. Even lightweight bristol board can be traced on in this manner.

FIG. 93. An image can be drawn larger or smaller by using a pantograph. This is a simple wooden or metal adjustable device with a place for a pointer and another for a pencil. With the pointer guided over the image, (center) the pencil reproduces (at right) the image to the size at which the pantograph is set.

FIG. 94. Another device, an optical instrument, which performs this same function is the "Prismascope", or its close relative, the "Camera Lucida." These instruments project an image from a flat or three-dimensional subject to the paper, and this image can be traced directly on the paper.

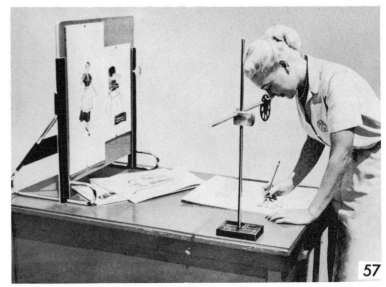

Fig. 94

Fig. 95

Cropping and Scaling

FIG. 95. So far we have considered the use of the entire photograph for reduction or enlargement. Suppose, on the other hand, we have an 8″ x 10″ photograph, and wish to select only a portion of the image and reduce this for insertion as a one column cut in a newspaper. FIG. 96. We have taken in only the area of the head and chest, including the medals. The procedure for cropping this area and scaling it to a 2″ width is illustrated on the following pages.

Fig. 96

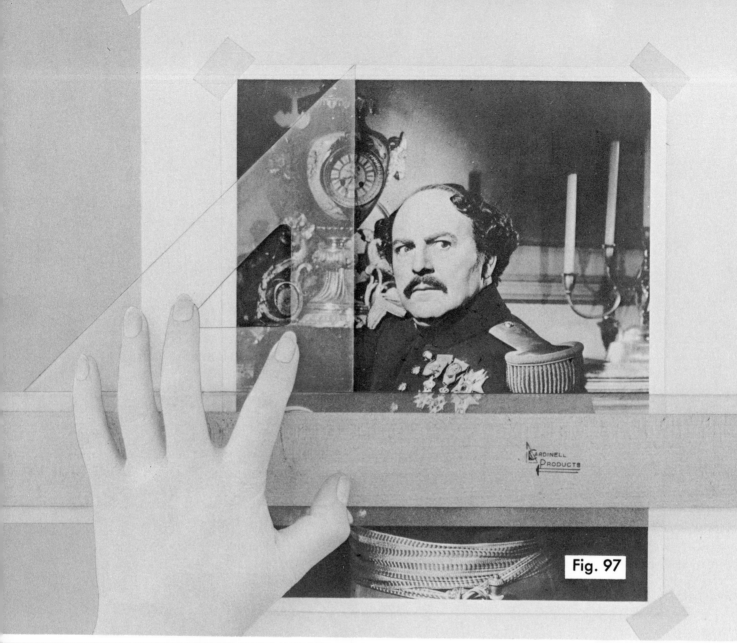

Fig. 97

Fig. 98

FIG. 97. First, line up the top of the photograph with the T-square, and tape the photo in position. Drop the T-square down to a convenient position and adjust the triangle at a place to the left of the head where it might be advisable to mark off the left hand margin of the area to be selected. It would not be advisable to crop too close to the head if a portion of the chest is to be shown.

FIG. 98. Using a white conte or grease pencil (since we are marking on a dark image), draw a vertical line from above the top of the head to below the medals.

FIG. 99. With the T-square in position, mark off a horizontal line just above the top of the head.

FIG. 100. Now from the left hand corner measure off the desired width of 1⅞″ on this horizontal.

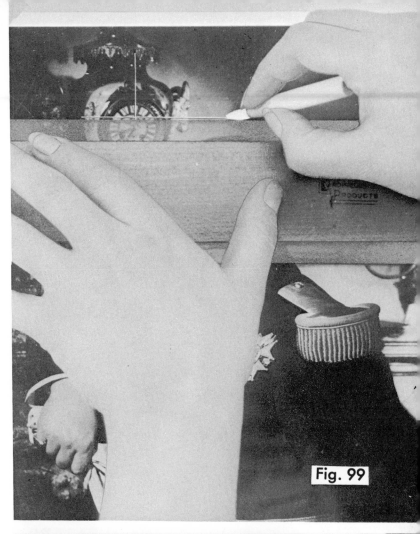

Fig. 99

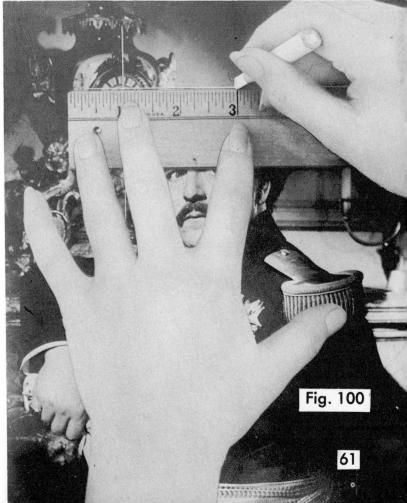

Fig. 100

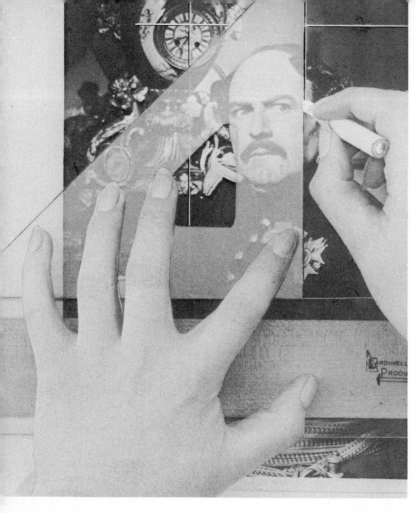

FIG. 101. From this point drop the vertical, using the T-square and triangle.

Fig. 101

FIG. 102. This shows what has been done up to this particular stage.

Fig. 102

FIG. 103. If we require a depth of 3″ in the reproduction, this is measured off the vertical, and,

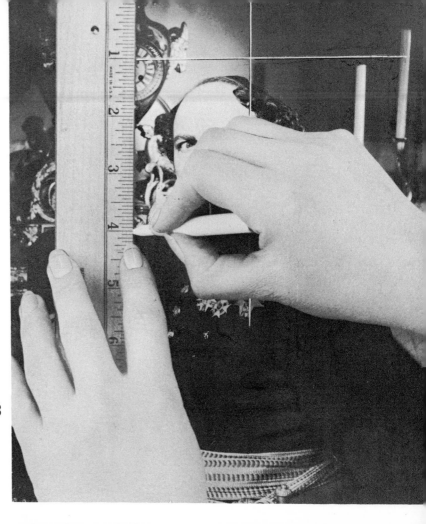

Fig. 103

FIG. 104, the bottom horizontal line is drawn through this point. We now have indicated on the photograph the left and top margins that will appear in the cropped and reduced image, and have defined the new size at which this image will be reproduced, but not the actual area it will take in. It is now necessary to determine what the right hand vertical margin and bottom horizontal margins will be, in scale with the rectangle shown.

Fig. 104

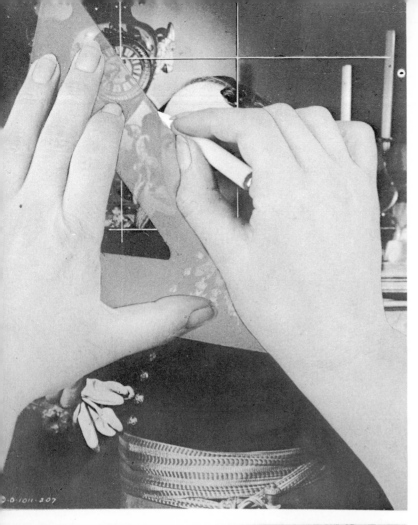

FIG. 105. This is achieved by first drawing a diagonal through this rectangle.

Fig. 105

FIG. 106. It will now be seen that we have the basis for marking off any portion of the image horizontally or vertically, and extending a line from it to the diagonal.

Fig. 106

FIG. 107. Since we may set our right hand margin at any convenient place, let's do it so that when a vertical is dropped to the diagonal it will meet it at a point (A) just below the medals.

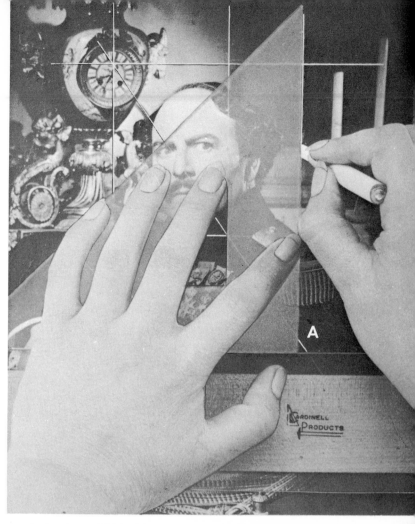

Fig. 107

FIG. 108. A line drawn from this point to the left hand vertical will now define the *area* (the outside rectangle) which will reduce to the *size* required (the inside rectangle), shown unobstructed in the next illustration.

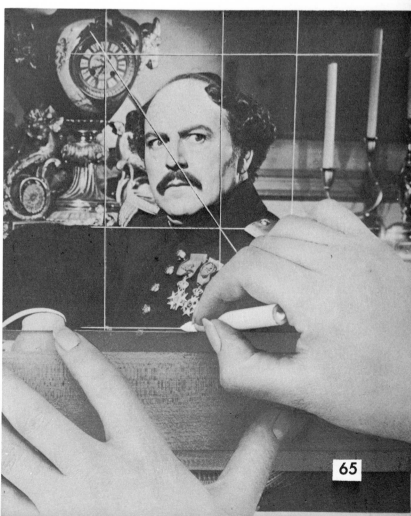

Fig. 108

Fig. 109

FIG. 109. To repeat, the inside rectangle represents the actual size at which the selected portion of the photo will reproduce; the outside rectangle represents the image area which will reduce to the size of the inside rectangle.

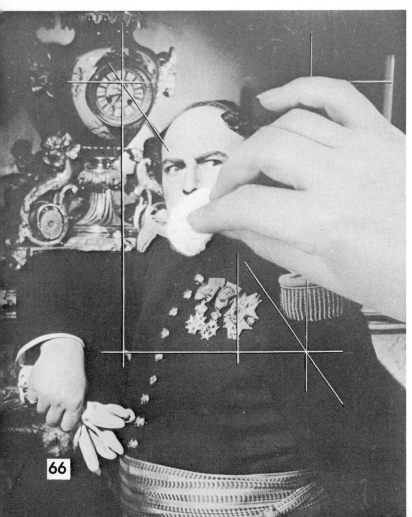

FIG. 110. Except for the trim marks in the corner, the scaling marks may now be eliminated by rubbing them off with cotton. (If the marks do not erase easily use cotton which has been lightly dipped in talcum powder. Remove the excess talcum powder with clean cotton). The trim marks can be used to indicate dimensions, as well as a cropping guide for the plate maker.

Fig. 110

FIG. 111. If the photograph is to be reproduced with a white background, that is as a silhouette, this can be indicated by drawing a white line with poster color around the area to be silhouetted. If the photograph is glossy there may be some difficulty making the poster color adhere to the surface. There are various mediums which when added to the poster color will make it easier to adhere to the surface of the photograph: e. g. Non-crawl, and Wetz.

Fig. 111

FIG. 112. The line should be at least 1/16″ thick, and cross marks put on the background that is to be eliminated. This will then be photographed to reduced size, as indicated, and the background eliminated by the engraver so that the image will appear in reproduction as shown.

Fig. 112

67

COMPOSITES

Making a Composite

FIG. 113. In this particular case, the problem consists of actually *cutting* silhouettes of the portrait images from two separate photographs, (both in the same scale), and making a composite of them on a 50 per cent gray background. The rough layout, FIG. 114, is provided as a guide for the artist, and indicates what is to be done with the photographs.

FIG. 115. A tracing made from the two photos, in their new desired position, will be used as a guide when pasting up.

FIG. 116. The figures are silhouetted by cutting out the background with a pair of scissors. Since these cutouts will be mounted on gray paper, it is necessary to cut close to the image so as not to leave the white paper outline around the figures when pasted on the gray ground. A razor blade can be used for this purpose also, in which case the cutting edge should be beveled inward towards the image to further decrease the possibility of leaving a line around the image.

FIG. 117. After the photograph is cut out, it is laid face down on a sheet of glass and the edges sandpapered until they are comparatively thin. This will remove irregular edges and decrease the possibility of the thickness of the photograph showing when pasted down on the gray paper. The sanding should be done gently, with a motion paralleling the edge of the image, to minimize the possibility of tearing the photograph.

Arrows show the direction in which the sandpaper is moved for these particular sections. The sandpaper which is used to point up pencils may be used for this purpose. It should not be too coarse and may be purchased in pads.

Fig. 113

Fig. 114

Fig. 115

Fig. 116

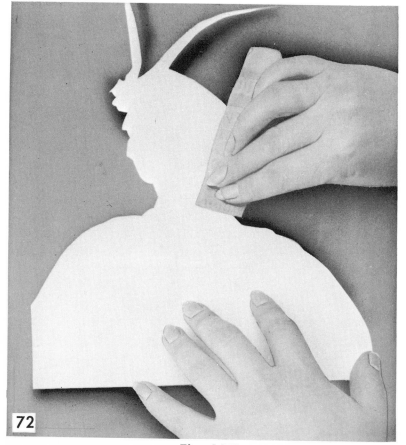

FIG. 118. After the sanding has eliminated any irregular and rough edges, the edges of the photograph are painted with opaque water color which matches the gray of the background. This further minimizes the edges of the photograph showing against the background. If the tone of the background were not of the same value throughout, it would be advisable to paint the edges of the photograph with tones which would match the various portions of the *image* rather than the background.

FIG. 119. Assuming that the gray paper has been mounted on a sheet of illustration board for rigidity, and that this gray paper and the backs of the photographs have been coated with rubber cement and allowed to dry, we are now ready to paste the photographs in position. The outline guide on tracing paper is taped in position over the gray paper, and a sheet of thin paper placed between this and the gray paper to prevent the photograph from adhering to the cemented surface immediately. The photograph can now be maneuvered into position using the overlay as a guide.

Fig. 117

Fig. 118

Fig. 119

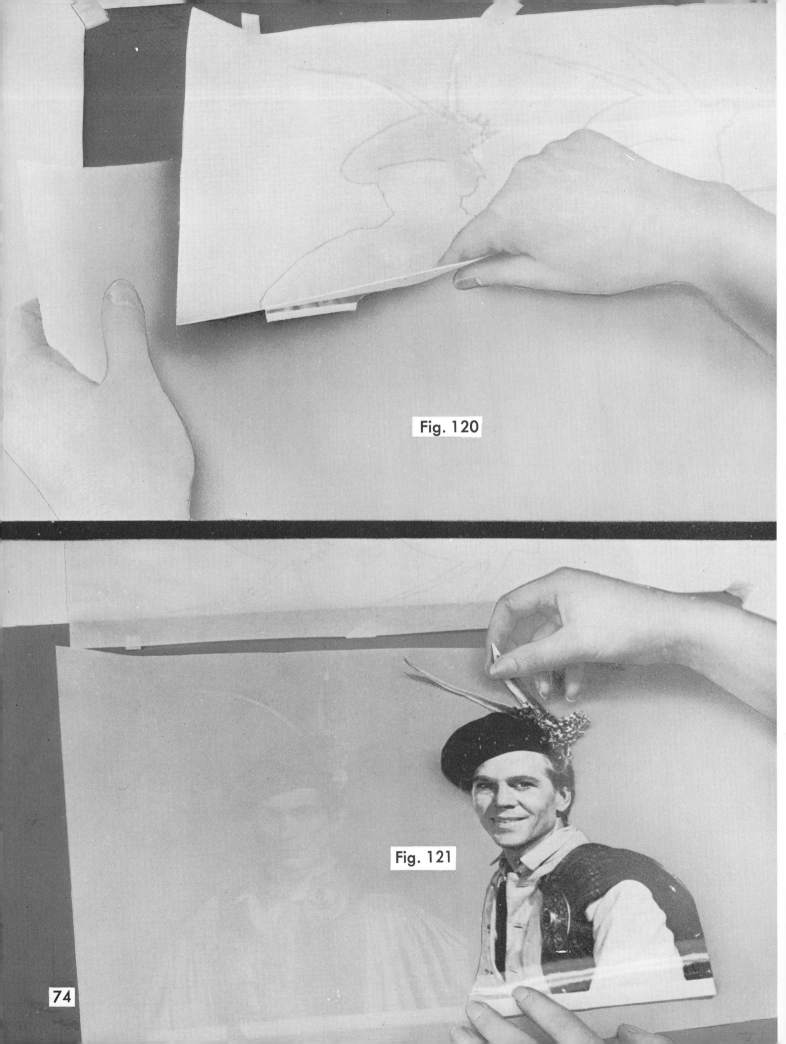

Fig. 120

Fig. 121

FIG. 120. When the photo has been properly located, the protecting tracing paper can be gradually slipped out from underneath it, allowing the photograph to adhere to the background. After the top edge of the photograph has stuck, check to see if the rest is in register before removing more of the protecting paper.

FIG. 121. The same is done with the other photograph. Note that the protecting sheet of paper has been again placed between the overlay guide and the background paper.

FIG. 122. The excess area at the bottom of the photographs is trimmed by cutting along a metal straight edge with a razor blade. Care must be taken not to cut too deeply or the gray paper will be marred, though actually this edge will not appear in the cropped reproduction.

FIG. 123. If the photograph has adhered to the background so strongly the excess portions cannot be removed without tearing, rubber cement thinner may be squeezed from a small oil can to dissolve the rubber cement, and allow the strip to be removed easily. This will not stain the photographs or artwork involved. The remaining rubber cement is removed from the background with a pick-up as shown on page 37.

Fig. 122

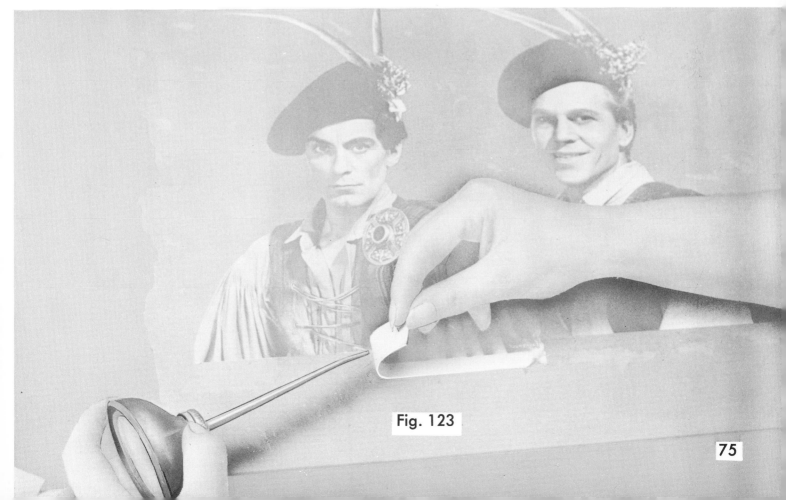

Fig. 123

75

Fig. 124

Fig. 125

FIG. 124. Any retouching, such as continuing the details in the feather, and separating edges from the background with line work, etc., may be performed at this stage. See page 129 for directions on retouching. The finished composite, ready for the plate maker, is shown in FIG. 125, with trim marks and dimensions. In FIG. 126 it is shown as it would appear in reproduction, with the area beyond the trim marks eliminated.

Fig. 126

Fig. 127

Fig. 128

Composite Plus Artwork

There are three problems involved in this particular composite: the pasteup of two separate photographs, FIGS. 127 and 128; flush mounting of one photograph against the second, as well as against a sheet of gray paper; and drawing artwork directly on the background paper. Since both photographs are in the same scale, it is possible to flush mount them together, otherwise it would be necessary to mount only one in the layout and merely indicate the position of the other photograph, and scale it separately as shown on page 42.

FIG. 129. The rough layout shows the positioning of the photographs and artwork. The procedure is shown on the following pages.

Fig. 129

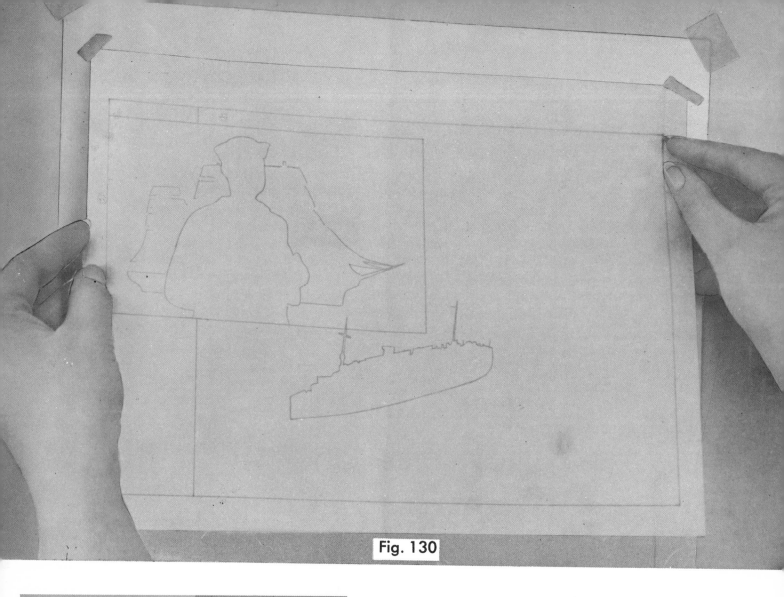

Fig. 130

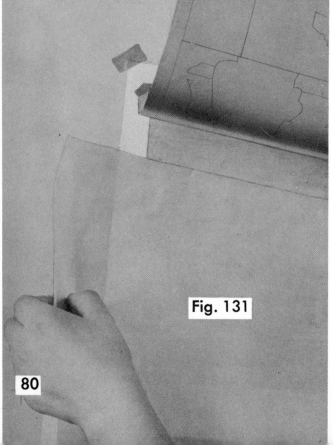

Fig. 131

FIG. 130. An accurate outline tracing of the photographs, the actual size of the layout, is first made to assure correct positioning. This tracing is laid over the illustration board on which the photographs are to be mounted and taped securely at the upper corners.

FIG. 131. The illustration board is covered with rubber cement, which is allowed to dry, and a sheet of tracing paper laid over this so that the large photograph, which has also been rubber cemented on the back, will not adhere immediately until it is positioned correctly.

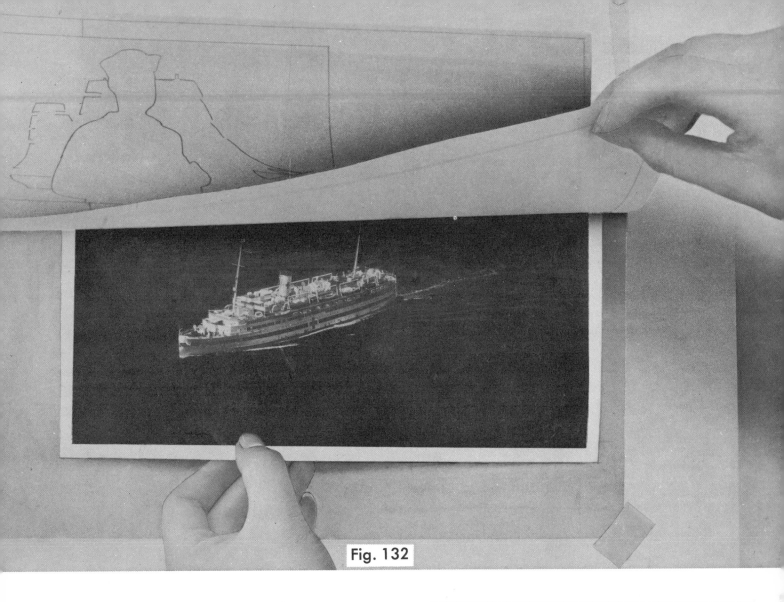

Fig. 132

FIG. 132. The large photograph is placed in position with the tracing paper overlay as a guide.

FIG. 133. When the traced outline of the ship is in register with the same image on the photograph, the protecting paper is slowly removed and the photograph allowed to adhere to the illustration board for about a quarter of an inch along its top edge.

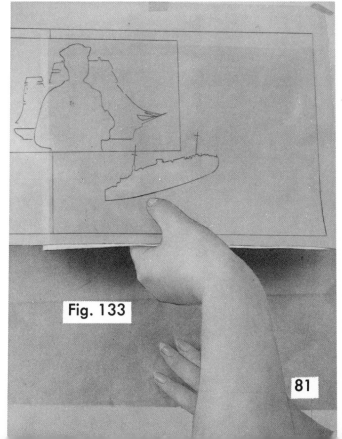

Fig. 133

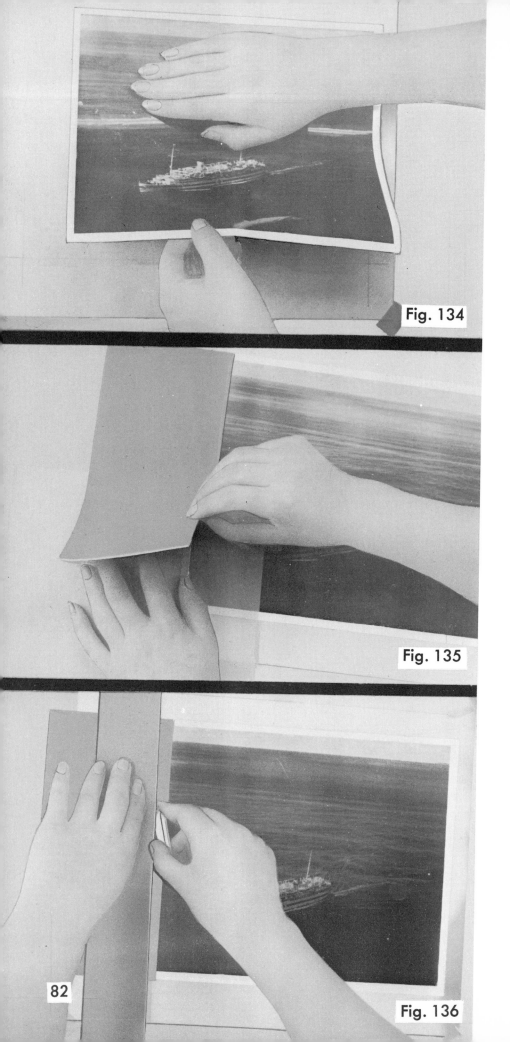

FIG. 134. Both the overlay and the protective sheet may now be removed and the photograph gradually pressed into position.

Fig. 134

FIG. 135. Next a sheet of gray color-aid paper at least one-half inch larger all around than the required size is rubber cemented on the back and placed lightly in position according to the layout.

Fig. 135

FIG. 136. Using the metal edge and razor blade, both the color-aid paper and photograph are now cut through in one stroke along the line indicated on the layout for their joining. This is done so that both the color-aid paper and the photograph may be mounted flush with no overlap.

Fig. 136

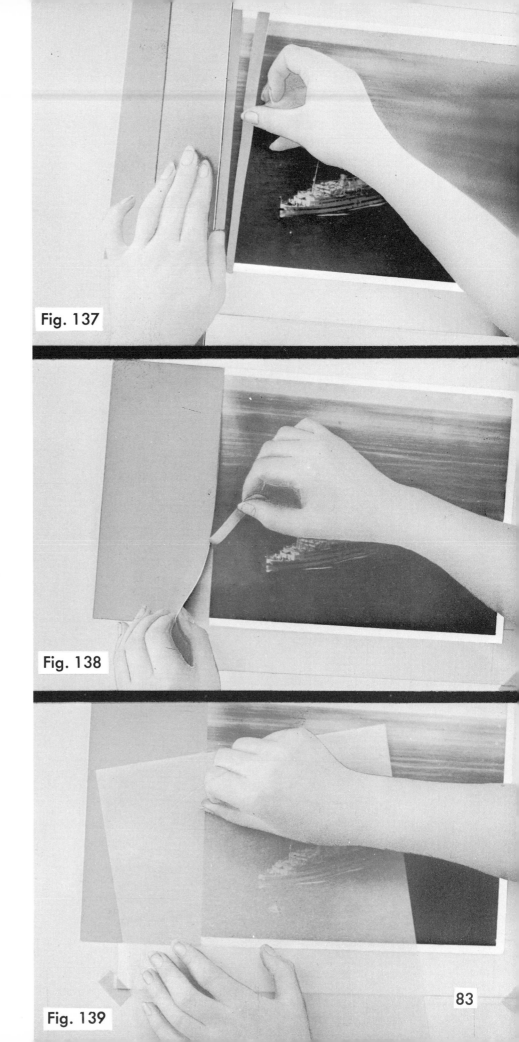

FIG. 137. The excess strip of color-aid paper is removed. This will come off easily, as no rubber cement was placed on the top surface of the photograph before the color-aid paper was placed on it.

Fig. 137

FIG. 138. The inside edge of the color-aid paper is now gently lifted along its entire length and the excess strip of photograph underneath it removed.

Fig. 138

FIG. 139. Using a sheet of tracing paper for protection, the cut edges are pressed down firmly with the thumbnail or a spoon.

83

Fig. 139

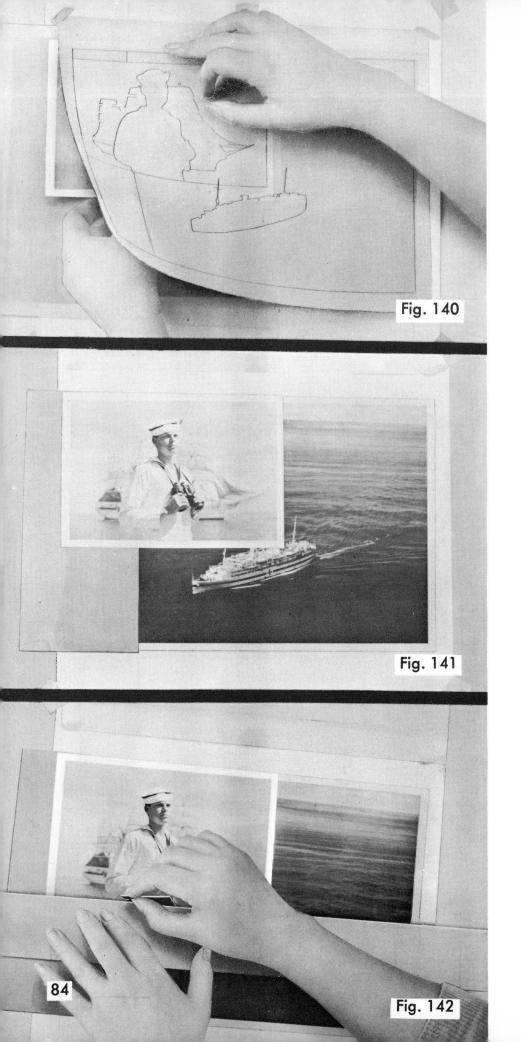

Fig. 140

Fig. 141

Fig. 142

FIG. 140. It is at this point that the difference in procedure occurs between ordinary mounting of the photos, and flush mounting. If the smaller photo were to remain *on top* of both the paper and large photo, rubber cement would be applied to all these surfaces at this stage. However, since the small photograph is to be *mortised into* the large photograph and color-aid paper, a wet coating of rubber cement on the back of the small photograph is sufficient to hold it in position until necessary mortising is done. The outline tracing is used to position this photograph also.

FIG. 141. This shows the photograph in position before being mortised. Note that the small photo has not been trimmed yet.

FIG. 142. Using the crop marks indicated on the top, sides and bottom of the layout as a guide, cut through the top photograph, and at the same time through the layers beneath it—that is, on the left of the color-aid paper, and on the right of the large photo. It is best to do this in one clean stroke on each cut—one each for top, bottom and each side. Do not cut beyond the area defined by the trim marks, but be sure that the vertical and horizontal cuts meet at the corners.

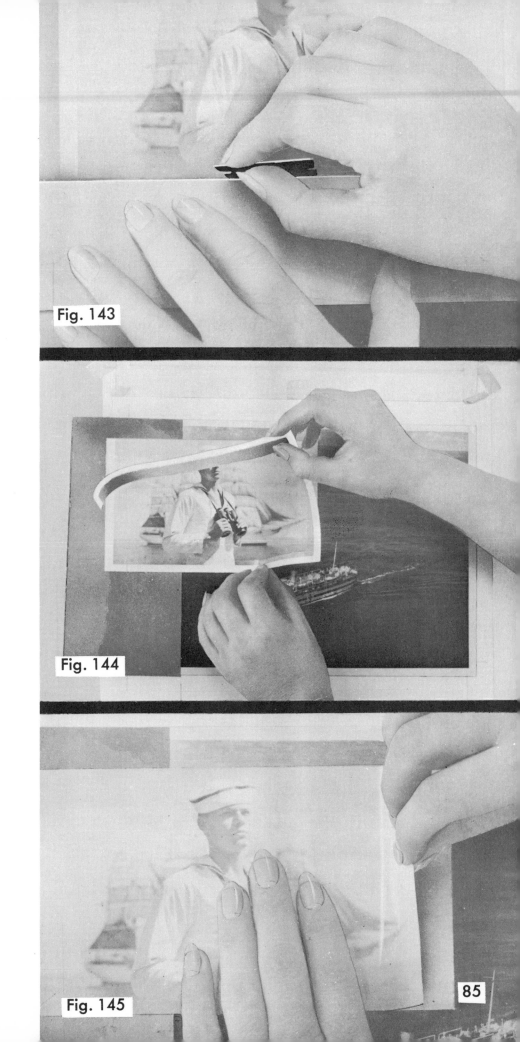

FIG. 143. An enlarged view of the previous illustration.

Fig. 143

FIG. 144. The excess margins of the small photograph are removed.

Fig. 144

FIG. 145. The right hand side of the small photograph is lifted — be certain not to shift the entire photograph, as it will disturb the accurate position. A knife blade slipped under the corner will facilitate lifting. This will expose the area of the large photograph underneath.

85

Fig. 145

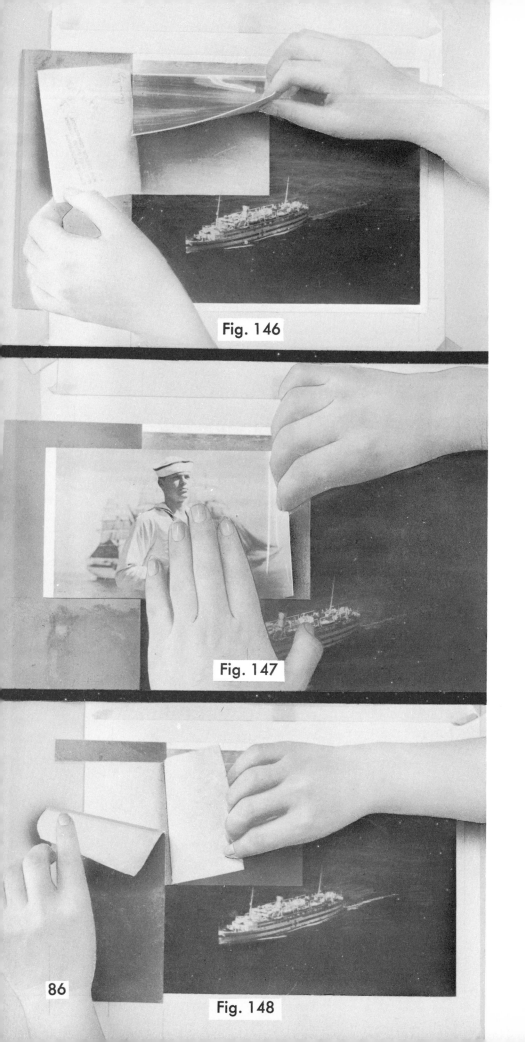

Fig. 146

Fig. 147

Fig. 148

FIG. 146. This exposed section of the large photograph which was previously cut through as explained in FIG. 142 is lifted carefully and removed.

FIG. 147. The small photograph is now replaced in position; since both photographs have been previously cut through at the same time, there will be no space or gap between the cut edges.

FIG. 148. The left hand side of the small photograph and the color-aid paper beneath it are treated in the same manner.

FIG. 149. Any excess rubber cement is removed carefully with masking tape or a pick-up.

FIG. 150. The artwork, in this case the anchor, is traced onto the color-aid paper, using light gray or white pastel as a backing for the transfer paper. Color-aid paper is soiled by erasure, so it must be handled with care. Any pastel remaining on the color-aid paper can be dusted off with a brush after the anchor has been painted in. The anchor is painted with light gray poster color.

FIG. 151. The completed composite.

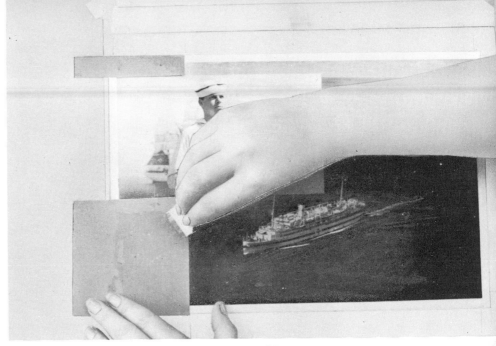

Fig. 149

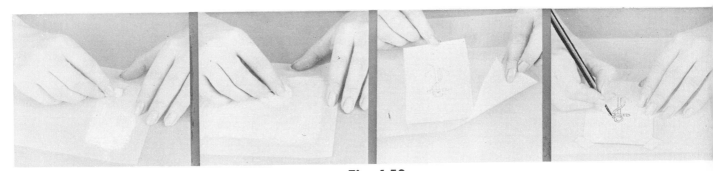

Fig. 150

Fig. 151

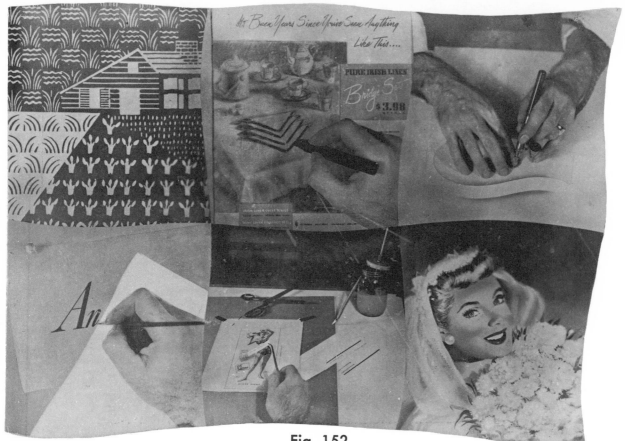

Fig. 152

|← —————— 6½" —————— →|

Fig. 153

REVERSE
THIS IS TO
BE WHITE

TOOLED OUT
OF HALFTON
PLATE

88

|← —————— 6½" —————— →|

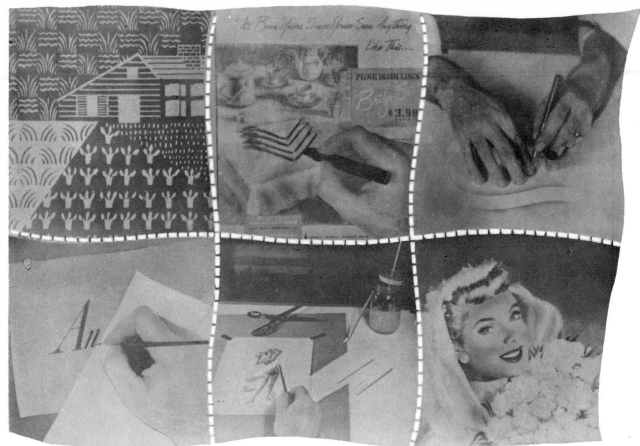

Fig. 154

FIG. 152. The procedure, just described, is here applied to a more complicated layout wherein six separate photographs are combined with curved, rather than straight line mortising, registered with a dotted white line, shown in finished reproduction, FIG. 154.

Only by mounting the photographs by the procedure described could they have been mounted with such accuracy. In this instance, the cutting lines would be drawn on tracing paper and used as a guide for placing the individual, cemented photographs in position, overlapping each other slightly. The cutting, would then be done through the tracing guide and photographs at the same time, the tracing guide having been cemented in position for this purpose. The tracing paper can be removed after the cutting operation and the procedure carried on as explained on page 86.

FIG. 153. In addition to the mortising, we now consider the manner in which the white dotted-line effect over the cut lines is achieved in reproduction. Needless to say, it would not be practical to paint or rule the lines directly on the cracks. A more efficient method is to rule solid lines with black ink on a sheet of acetate or tracing paper placed over the layout, then to cut across the lines with a brush with white poster color. This dotted line overlay is then indicated for reversal. The photo-engraver effects the change during the photographic stage of plate-making.

Pasteup with Borders

This might be a typical editorial pasteup job wherein it is necessary to crop the subjects carefully from photographs which contain other material, paste them in position, and divide them with narrow strips of gray tone. The rough layout is shown in FIG. 155. The various photographs from which the material is to be cropped are shown in FIG. 156. They are all in the same scale, so they can all be placed directly into position on the mechanical.

If not all in the same scale, they could have been handled as shown in the mechanical on page 151.

From the rough, an accurate pencil layout is made. From this a tracing slightly larger in depth, but smaller in width than the rectangular shape of one of the individual panels is made to serve as a guide in cutting the individual photos.

FIG. 157. This tracing is shifted over the shell to determine the best location of the shell in the panel. When this is determined, a pushpin is used to make a slight hole through the tracing photograph in each corner. The photo is then trimmed to this size with a razor blade or scissors, using the corner holes as guides. Each photo is treated in this manner, and these are pasted in position. The layout calls for a gray border or narrow separation between each

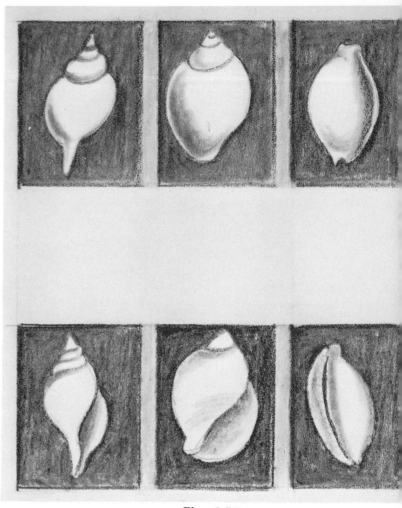

Fig. 155

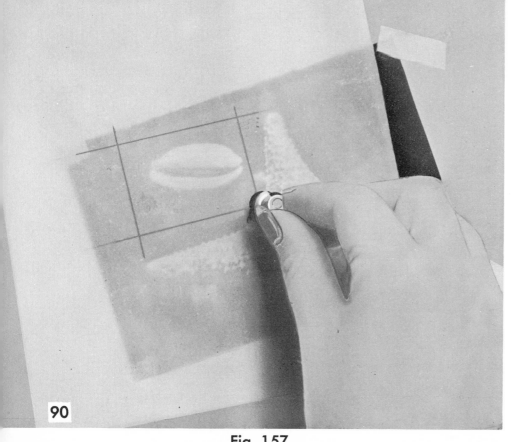

90

Fig. 157

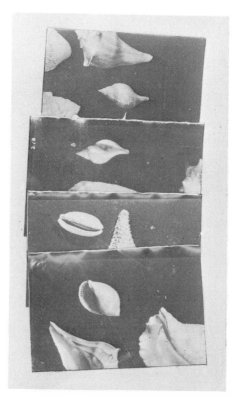

Fig. 156

photo. It would have been possible to do this by first painting gray strips on the paper, then fitting the photographs in place; but it is much more convenient and accurate to cut paper strips the width required and paste them over the photos, allowing them to overlap the photos slightly so that there will be no break in the straight lines.

FIG. 158. Color-aid paper, which is obtainable in various shades of gray, may be cut out and used for this purpose. An accurate and convenient method is to use an adjustable dual line cutter, as illustrated.

FIG. 159. The strips of gray are pasted in position. The rubber cement need only be used on the back of the paper strips in this instance, and applied wet. Since the photos were made slightly larger in depth, the excess sections can be trimmed in single strokes horizontally across the tops and bottoms of each panel, including the border strips, and removed. This will provide perfect alignment of these edges. Any excess rubber cement should be cleaned off.

FIG. 160. The finished mechanical is shown actual size.

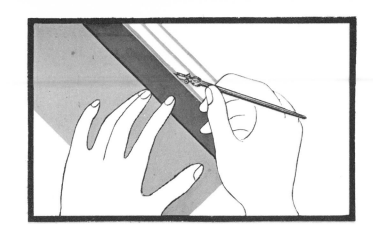

Fig. 158

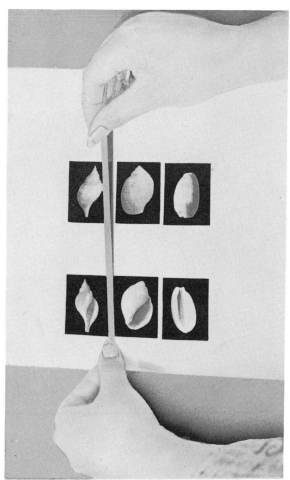

Fig. 159

Fig. 160

Pasteup Lettering

In advertising and publication work, lettering is obtained by several means: (1) hand lettering (2) printed type (3) photographic lettering (4) pasteup lettering. On the next page, examples of pasteup lettering are illustrated. This is lettering obtainable in various type faces, printed on clear acetate sheets, the backs of which have an adhesive, either of rubber cement or of wax. The individual letters required are cut out and pasted in position to form necessary words. This is done as a convenience, or an economy measure, or for special effects. Pasteup letters are obtainable in a multitude of type faces: in Roman, block, script, shaded, calligraphic and novelty forms; both in black letters for use on white backgrounds, FIG. 161, or in white letters for use on black or gray backgrounds as shown in FIG. 162. The particular pasteup types shown have a waxed backing. It will be noted in the reverse lettering that the areas surrounding the A's, E's, 3's, and O's are darker than the rest of the sheet. This is due to the fact that the waxed backing becomes more transparent after it is pressed into contact with the black paper, as in this particular case. In other words, to illustrate this point the remaining areas of the sheet intentionally have not been pressed fully in contact with the black paper and, therefore remain less transparent.

aaaaabbbcccdddeeeeeee
ffgghhhhhiiiijjjkkllllm
mmnnnnnooooopppq
qrrrrsssssstttttuuuu
vvwwxxyyzz$$1122
33445566778899000

CRAFTYPE H-3-2-96I THE CRAFTINT MFG. CO.
Pat. No. 2206203 Cleveland 10, Ohio.

Fig. 161

In addition to type faces, various symbols used in technical illustrations and in chart and map-making are obtainable, as are various graphic aids such as dotted lines, circles, register marks, dots, etc.

H-3-2-96I
Pat. No. 2206203

aaaaabbbcccdddeeeeeee
ffgghhhhhiiiijjjkkllllm
mmnnnnnooooopppq
qrrrrsssssstttttuuuu
vvwwxxyyzz$$1122
33445566778899000

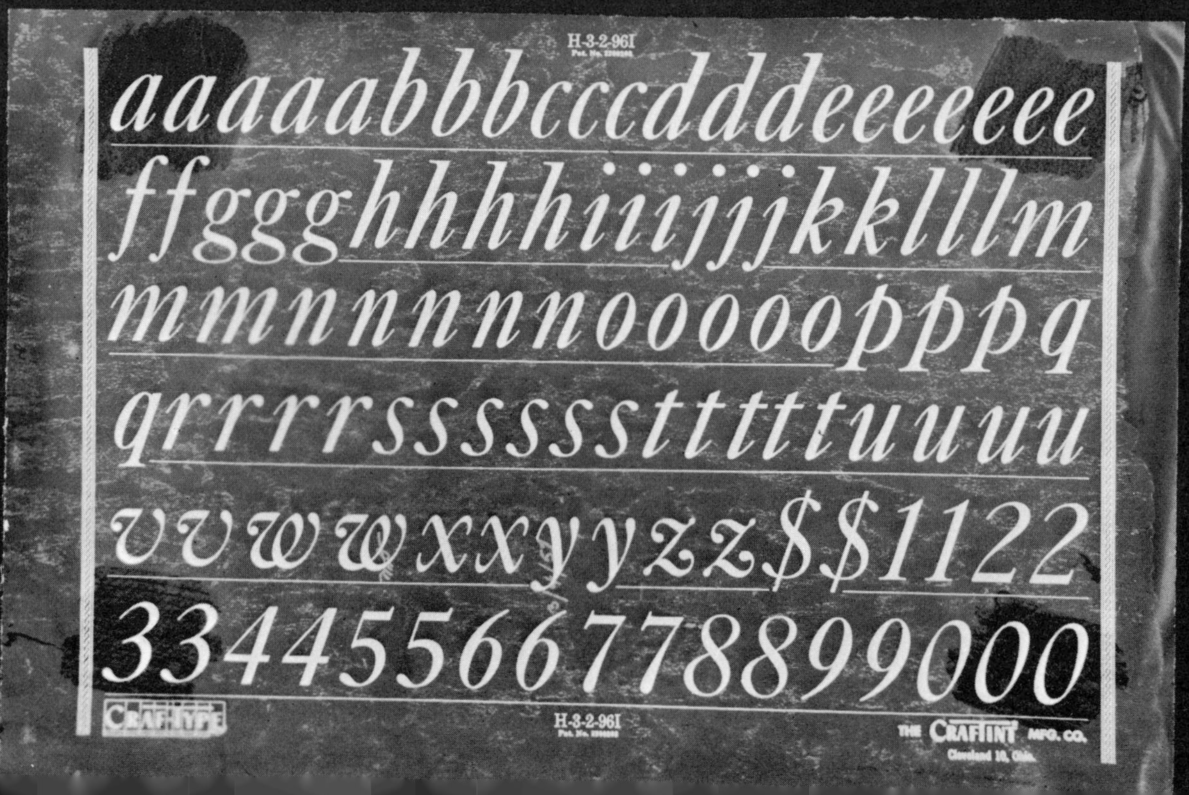

CRAFTYPE H-3-2-96I THE CRAFTINT MFG. CO.
Pat. No. 2206203 Cleveland 10, Ohio.

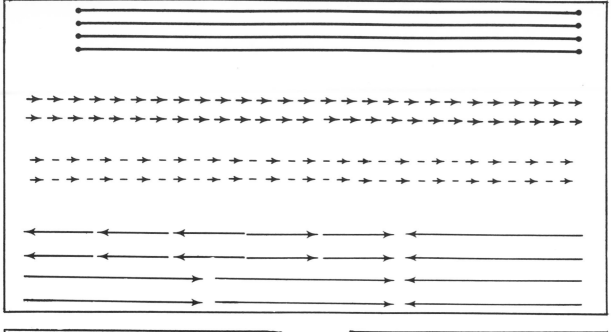

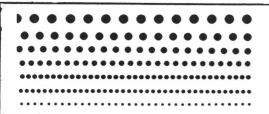

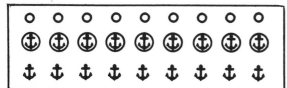

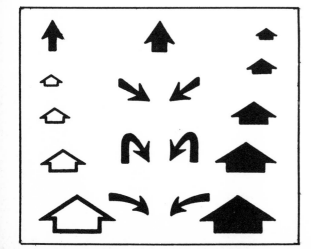

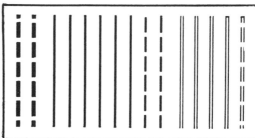

Fig. 163

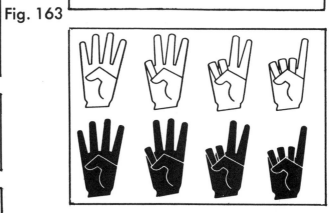

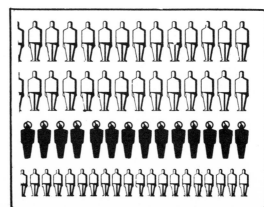

Fig. 164

Application of Pasteup Lettering

Let us follow through on a problem requiring the use of pasteup lettering. The particular pasteup lettering we are using in this instance is on thin paper stock instead of acetate, a form in which it is also available.

FIG. 164 shows the layout, a banner bearing the curved words "Telescopic Pete Ipana Clown". Though shown in reduced size here, the original layout on tracing paper is the actual size of the lettering job, reproduced on the next page.

FIG. 165. The individual letters are cut from the paper sheet (or the acetate) as indicated. Note that there is a guide line below each line of letters. This guide line is cut out with the letter placed in register with a guide line previously drawn on the illustration board on which the letters are to be mounted.

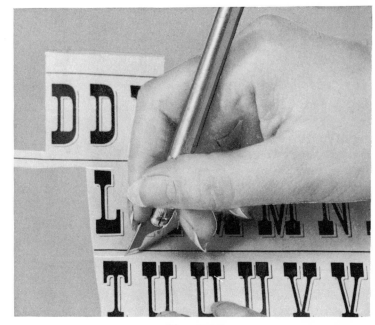

Fig. 165

FIG. 166. A letter is being pasted in position with its guide line placed in register with the previously drawn guide line on the illustration board. In this particular instance, the guide line on the board is curved, whereas the guide line below the letters is straight. Nevertheless, the line below the letter is so short that it can be placed in register with the curved line.

FIG. 167. After the letters are placed in position, the lower portion containing the guide line is cut through and removed so that the guide line will not reproduce. If it is not possible to cut it off, it may be opaqued out with white show-card color.

FIG. 168 shows the assembled letters pasted up and in position.

This was photographed so that the pasteup edges would show for instruction purposes. However, in straight black and white reproduction (line reproduction) these edges would drop out or could be opaqued out on the negative.

FIG. 169. The particular job illustrated here was required for reverse printing, that is, white lettering on a black background; and this reversal has been achieved by photostating the pasteup assembly and securing a negative photostat. This might also have been done by using white pasteup letters but they were not available in the particular form used, though they are available on acetate. Also this version shows a slight reduction from the original; if pasteup letters are not obtainable in the exact size required, they can either be enlarged or reduced by photostats after assembly. Often the same artwork is required for use in various sizes, and photostating the original art would serve the purpose, as illustrated by the various sized illustrations on page 126.

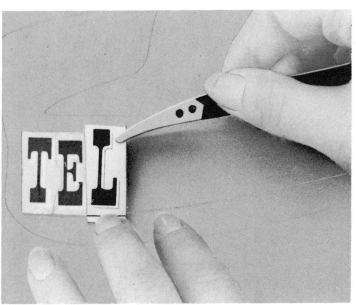

Fig. 166

Fig. 167

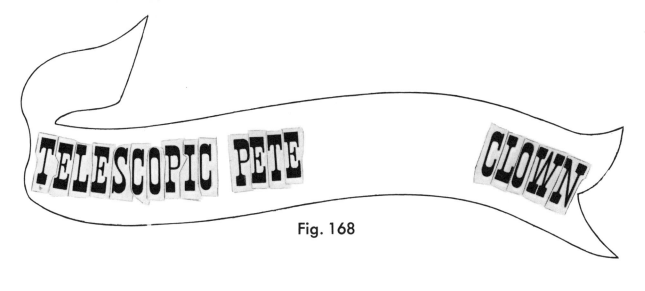

Fig. 168

Fig. 169

Fig. 170

98

Fig. 171

Pasteup lettering applied to greeting cards design provides an excellent opportunity for variety. FIG. 170 shows the original pasteup, and FIG. 171 as it appeared on the greeting card. FIG. 172 shows various types of lettering as they were pasted up, and FIG. 173 shows one verse as it was laid line for line after individual letters and words were assembled, as shown in the previous illustration.

Graduated! Volumes of

Good Wishes for a Happy

Future

A word to the wise
Congratulations and
Best Wishes for a
successful future
Flying the coop? will miss you
like the dickens but hope
you have good pickins!
Devoted! - But belated
hope you had a Happy Birthday
Let's face it you're the fairest of
them all

Fig. 172

Flying the coop?

will miss you

like the dickens

Fig. 173

but hope

you have

good pickins!

USE OF DRAFTING

AND DRAWING INSTRUMENTS

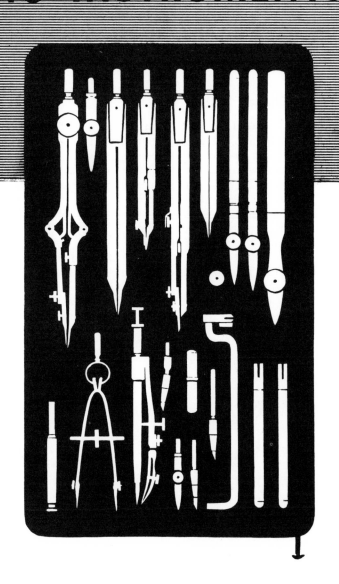

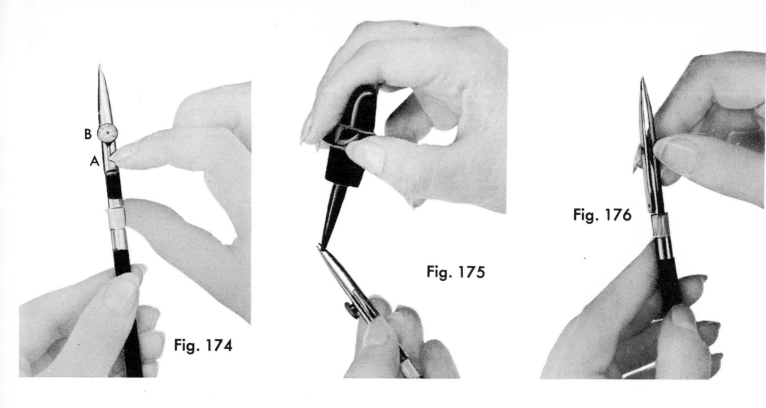

Fig. 174

Fig. 175

Fig. 176

Use of Ruling Pen

FIG. 174. The ruling pen is used to draw mechanically straight or curved lines, usually with india ink, although it can be used with colored inks, dyes, or opaque water color. There are different types of ruling pens for various uses, but the type shown here is generally used. Within a narrow range, it is adjustable for different thicknesses of line. In use, the pen is held like a pencil with the end of the index finger placed in the depression (A) which is on the same side of the pen as the adjusting screw (B).

FIG. 175. The pen is filled with ink from a dropper usually supplied with the ink bottle. Only a small amount of ink should be squeezed between the blades of the pen, as an excess amount will cause the ink to blot or run.

FIG. 176. The blades are adjusted for the thickness of line desired. Tightening the adjusting screw brings the blades closer together for a fine line; loosening it allows the blades to spread apart for a thicker line.

FIG. 177. After filling, the outside edges of the blades may be soiled with ink, which should be removed gently with the finger or a piece of blotting paper.

FIG. 178. Test the pen on a piece of scrap paper to determine if it is adjusted to the proper thickness of line and also to see that the ink is flowing properly. If the line is not of required

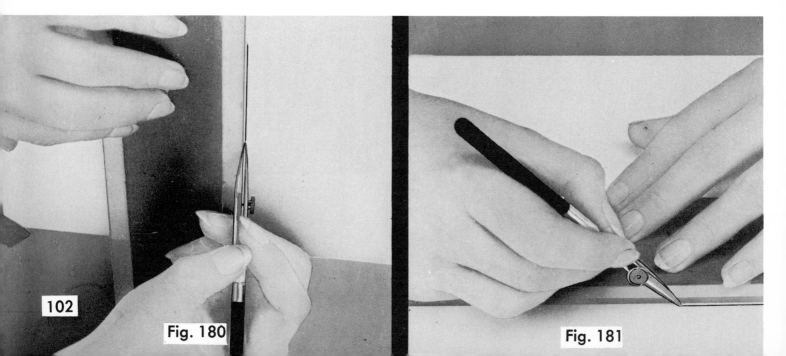

Fig. 180

Fig. 181

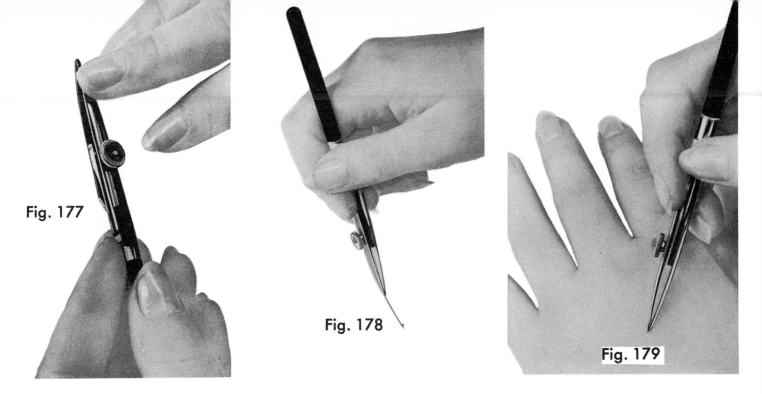

Fig. 177

Fig. 178

Fig. 179

thickness, adjust the pen until it is.

FIG. 179. If the ink does not flow easily, rub it across the back of the hand, as this generally starts the ink flowing.

FIG. 180. Straight lines are ruled either against a T-square edge, a ruler or a triangle. Straight lines are not ruled free-hand with a ruling pen, nor should the pen be used to fill in solid areas. Use a brush for this purpose. Note that the pen is held in a vertical plane when viewed from this particular angle. The pen should not wobble while the line is being drawn, otherwise the line itself will be wavy. Note also that there is a slight space between the line and the edge of the T-square. Do not allow the ink line to come flush up against the edge which is guiding it, as the ink will then flow underneath the edge.

FIG. 181. Viewed head on, we note that the pen may be inclined in the other plane, perhaps not as much as shown here.

FIG. 182. India ink has a tendency to dry rather rapidly in the pen. When this happens, unclog it by inserting the edge of a thin piece of paper between the blades and drawing it out through the end.

FIG. 183. The pen can be cleaned after use by using a cotton swab on the pointed end of the handle of a brush. The blades can be cleaned with water or with alcohol. Commercial pen cleaning solutions are also available. This particular type of pen is made with a blade which opens up for handy cleaning.

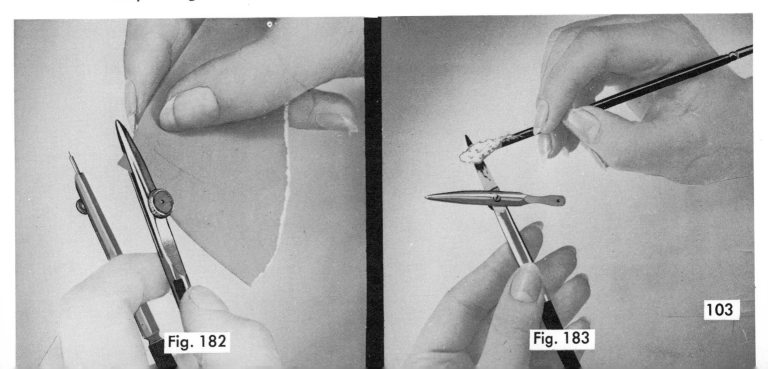

Fig. 182

Fig. 183

103

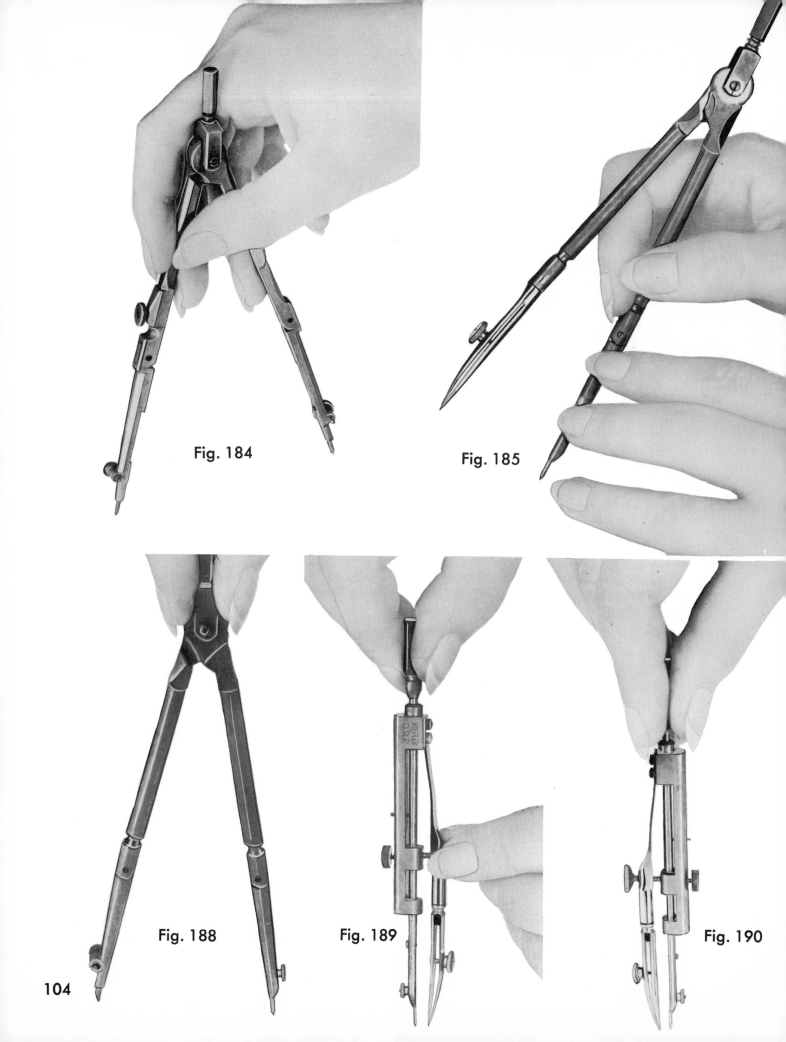

Fig. 184

Fig. 185

Fig. 188

Fig. 189

Fig. 190

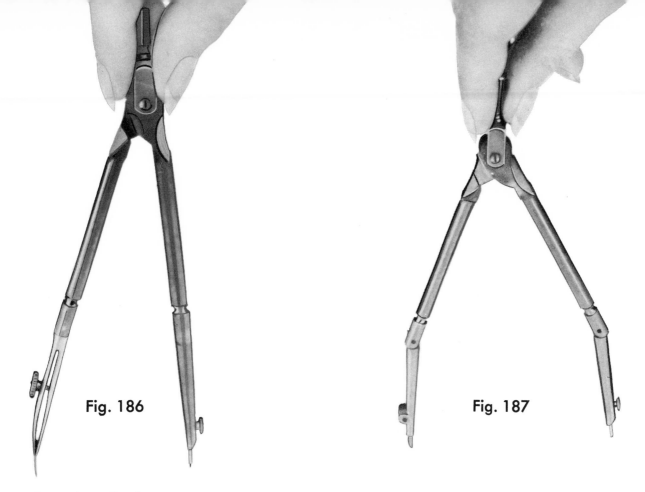

Fig. 186   Fig. 187

Drawing Circles

FIG. 184. In use, the compass point is first inserted into the paper and, by using the thumb and index finger on the free leg, and the third finger on the stationary leg, the compass can be easily adjusted to proper radius with one hand. The same method applies for dividers. (Dividers have points at the end of both legs instead of a pen or a pencil, and are used to mark off dimensions or linear divisions by pricking the paper with the points.) This drafting compass has an interchangeable leg for use as pencil, as shown, or a pen, next illustration.

FIG. 185. When setting the compass point at a specific spot, the compass can be steadied with the left hand and guided to its position for better accuracy. FIG. 186. After the point has been inserted in the paper and the compass adjusted to its proper radius, it should be held between the thumb and index finger by the gnarled extension at the top, and the circle drawn by twirling the compass slowly between these two fingers while leaning it over slightly at an angle towards the drawing or marking leg, as shown here with the pen, and, FIG. 188, with the pencil. FIG. 187. For circles of wider radius, the legs of the compass are bent so that they are almost vertical to the paper. When used in this manner, the compass is less likely to open up while drawing, and a better line is obtained by having the drawing edge in this position. FIG. 189. For very small circles, a drop compass is used. This allows for accurate and minute changes in the radius of a circle and also is made in such manner that the marking point (pencil or pen) can be raised for positioning the compass, and for adjusting to the required radius, as indicated. FIG. 190. When the required radius is obtained, the marking leg of the compass may be dropped in position and the circle made by holding the top of the compass with the thumb and index finger and twirling the compass. FIG. 191. For very large circles, a beam compass is used.

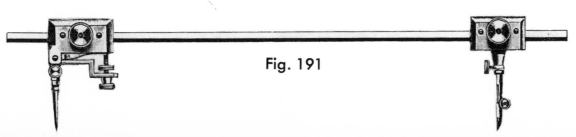

Fig. 191

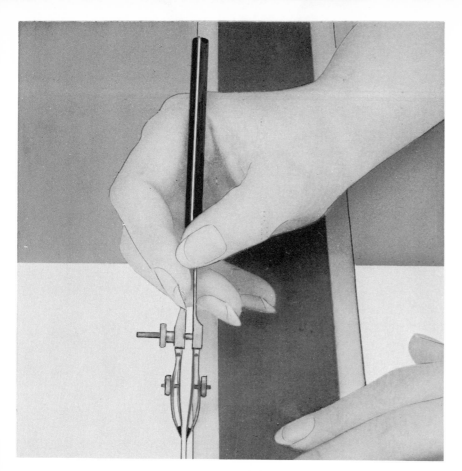

Fig. 192

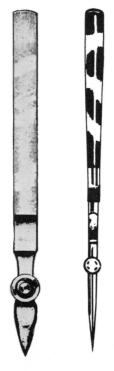

Fig. 194

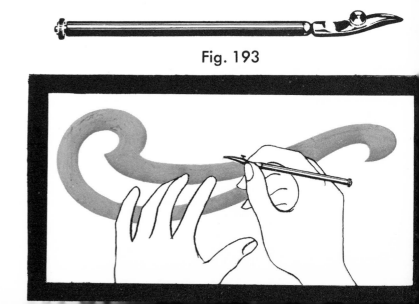

Fig. 193

FIG. 192. Special pens are obtainable for specific types of work. The one illustrated here is called a railroad pen and consists of two points on one pen, for drawing two parallel lines with one stroke. Space between the lines can be adjusted, as well as the thickness of the lines. If necessary to make the line solid, it can be filled in with a brush, *not* with a pen.

FIG. 193. Various types of pens are made, such as this swivel type, for ruling curved lines, and FIG. 194, a pen for ruling extra thick lines and one for very thin lines.

FIG. 195. The pen shown is a Wrico pen, which is a plunger type instrument with a well at the writing end, for use with india ink or thin opaque water color, or dyes. The pens are made in various sizes as each pen will only draw a line of specific thickness. Such a pen will follow any curved guide such as an ellipse guide, or french curve, without blotting.

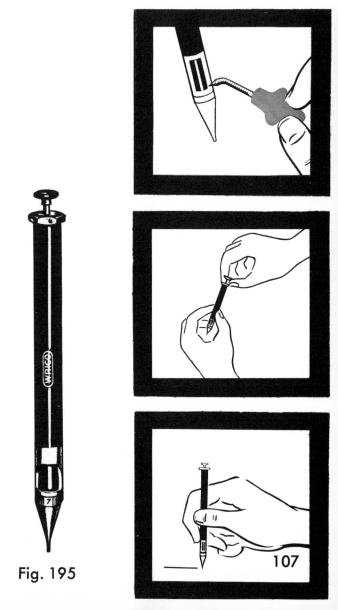

Fig. 195

107

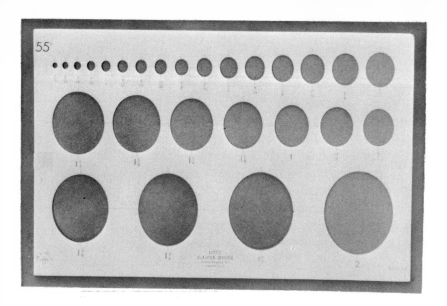

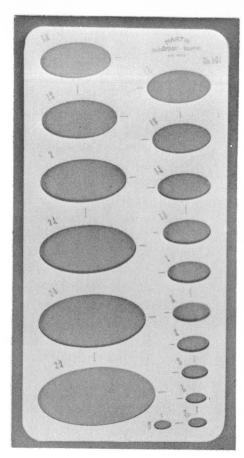

Fig. 196

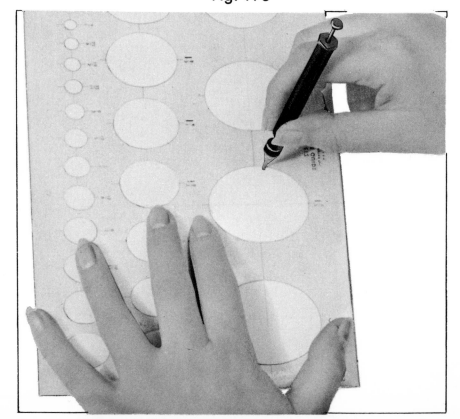

Fig. 198

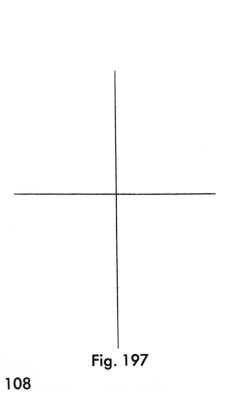

Fig. 197

Drawing Ellipses

FIG. 196. Ellipses can be drawn by using the compass in various positions. However ellipse guides or templates, of acetate, are made with cut-out ellipses in various sizes and various degrees of perspective, as shown.

FIG. 197. To draw an ellipse with such a guide, the vertical and horizontal axes of the ellipse are first drawn on the paper in the position where the ellipse is needed, then FIG. 198, the ellipse of proper size and perspective is selected and placed in register with the vertical and horizontal axes. If a penciled ellipse is desired, the pencil is placed inside the cutout and the ellipse circumscribed by following the edge. If an ink line is desired, it must be drawn with a Wrico, Inkograph, Leroy or similar pen, as it is not possible to use a ruling pen for this purpose except for very large ellipses.

FIG. 199. This shows the inked ellipse as drawn from the ellipse guide in the previous illustration.

FIG. 200. If concentric ellipses are desired, the next larger or smaller size is positioned over the same axes lines as was previously done and the larger ellipse drawn.

FIG. 201. It is advisable to draw the smaller one first and the larger one afterwards, as this lessens the chance of blotting the first ellipse drawn.

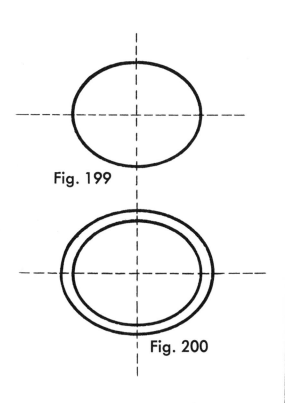

Fig. 199

Fig. 200

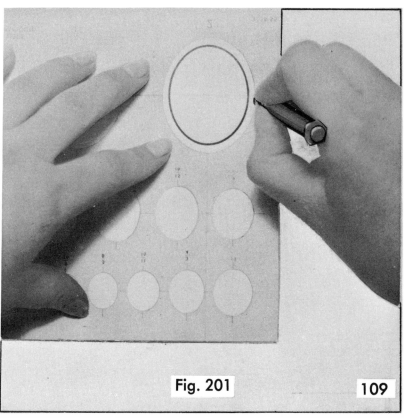

Fig. 201

360°

Fig. 202

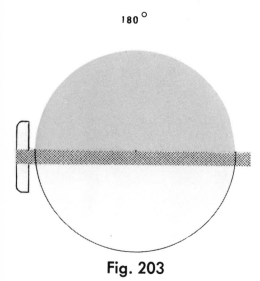

180°

Fig. 203

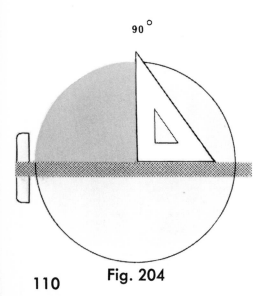

90°

Fig. 204

Angles, Degrees and Sectors

In making diagrams, graphs and various illustrations or layouts, it is often necessary to divide a circle into various proportions, or to determine specific angles.

A complete circle, FIG. 202, is made up of 360 degrees. This area is represented by the gray tone. Whether the circle is a small one or a large one it still is made up of 360 degrees.

FIG. 203. If we divide the circle in half by drawing a horizontal through its center with a T-square or ruler, each half will consist of 180 degrees. The upper half of 180 degrees is represented by the gray tone.

FIG. 204. Dividing the circle into a quarter area will give a 90 degree section. This is done by passing the T-square or ruler through the center of the circle, then adjusting the right triangle to this center point. The upper portion of the circle is divided into a 90 degree gray section, and a 90 degree white section (which includes the triangle). The bottom half section consists of 180 degrees. Thus other sections of various degrees can be obtained by dividing the circle proportionately.

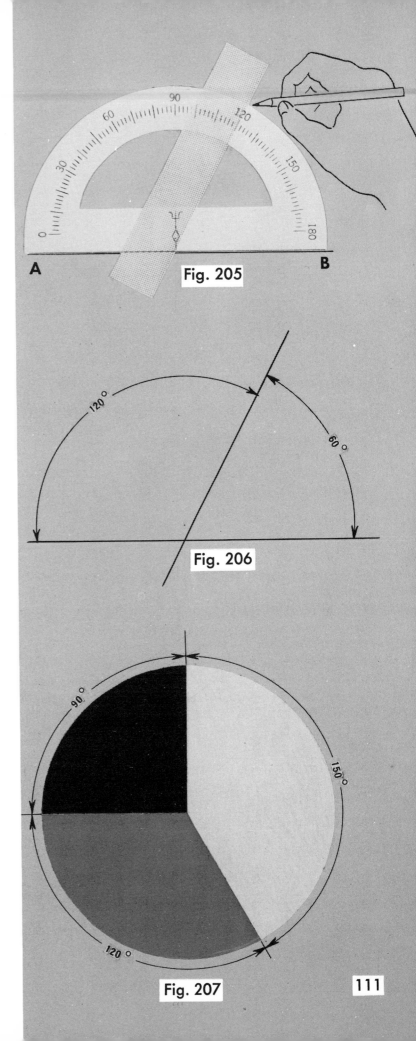

Fig. 205

Fig. 206

Fig. 207

Another method of obtaining angles of various degrees is by use of the protractor, FIG. 205. Drawing a line, AB, where the base of the angle is desired, place the marker of the protractor on this line at a point where the apex of the angle is to be located, then place a ruler through this point and the mark on the scale of the protractor the number of degrees desired, in this case, 120 degrees.

FIG. 206. Note that since the horizontal line represents 180 degrees, and we have cut an angle of 120 degrees across it, the remaining section represents the difference between the two, or 60 degrees. Most protractors are made with two scales so that angles can be read from either the left or the right side of the protractor.

FIG. 207 shows a circle divided into three portions, of 90, 150 and 120 degrees respectively.

In giving information for a graph or diagram, proportions could be provided in degrees, as considered; or in percentages, or in fractions. Suppose we are told that a given group of students fall into three categories; one-half of one type, one-third of another and one sixth of still another; and these three groups are to be portrayed graphically by sections of a circle. Since the complete circle is made up of 360 degrees, one half of this would be 180 degrees, one third would be 120 degrees and one sixth would be 60 degrees. Percentages such as 50%, 33-1/3%, and 16-2/3% are merely another way of expressing fractions, such as 1/2, 1/3 and 1/6 respectively, and so would be handled in the same manner.

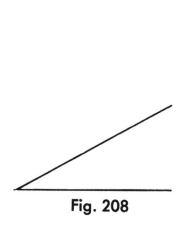

Fig. 208

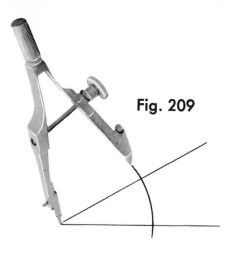

Fig. 209

Duplicating an Angle

FIG. 208. An angle which already is drawn, can be measured with a protractor and duplicated elsewhere as needed. An angle can also be duplicated by other methods.

FIG. 209. For example, place the point of a compass at the apex of the angle and swing an arc through both sides of the angle, then, FIG. 210, with the same compass setting swing this arc through the base of the new angle at the place where it is required.

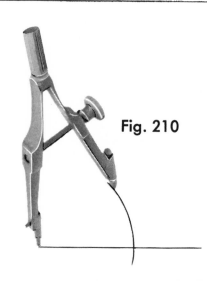

Fig. 210

FIG. 214. A very simple and comparatively accurate method of duplicating an angle, is to place a piece of paper over it, FIG. 215, with one edge of the paper on line with the apex of the angle (B). Mark a pencil dot on the paper at B, and on the opposite edges of the angle where the sides extend. Markings are

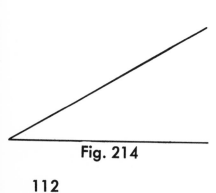

Fig. 214

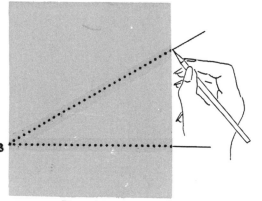

Fig. 215

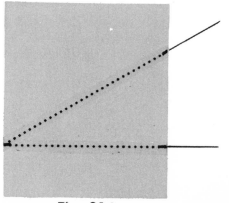

Fig. 216

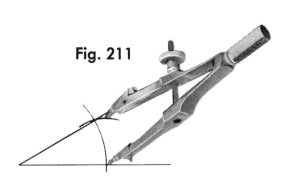

Fig. 211

FIG. 211. Now return to the original angle. Place the compass point where the arc meets the base and, adjusting the compass opening until it passes through the other intersection of the arc, draw another short arc at this point. Retaining this same compass setting, measure off the arc on the new angle, FIG. 212, then complete the new angle by drawing a line from point B to the intersection of the arcs. FIG. 213 shows the angle with construction marks erased.

Fig. 212

Fig. 213

B

B

shown in FIG. 216. The paper is transferred to the line on which the new angle is to be duplicated, FIG. 217, the markings repeated, the paper removed, FIG. 218, and the angle drawn through the points, FIG. 219.

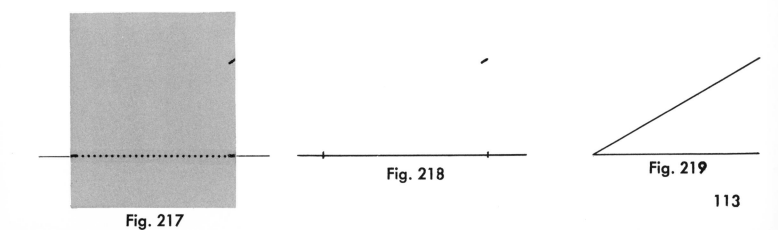

Fig. 218

Fig. 219

Fig. 217

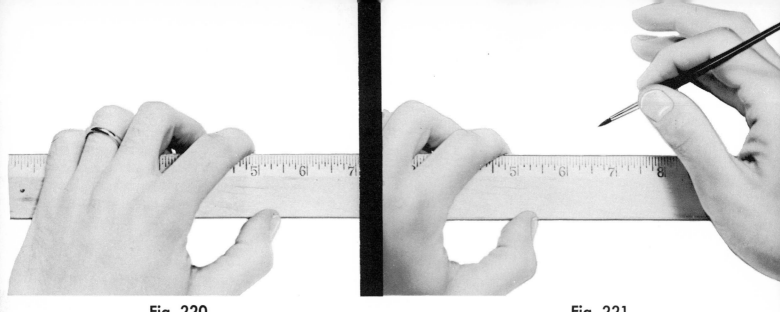

Fig. 220   **Fig. 221**

Ruling Straight Lines

While possible, it is not always convenient or advisable to rule a straight line with paint in a drawing pen. This especially applies where the line is being drawn on a surface which already has been airpainted with watercolor. There is always the possibility of the line spreading on the painted surface, especially if the paint in the pen is too thin. The sable brush, used with a ruler, is faster because there is no need to change over to the pen, with its consequent adjusting, cleaning, etc. Also, it allows more control in making straight lines of varying thickness, and small curved lines, using opaque color.

FIG. 220. A fairly thick ruler with a metal edge is advisable. It should be grasped in the left hand, with only the base of the ruler in contact with the paper, the top raised to an angle of about 30 degrees. This position is better shown in the side-view, FIG. 225.

FIG. 221. Be certain that the ruler is level and in firm contact with the paper. Hold the brush between thumb and index finger of the right hand.

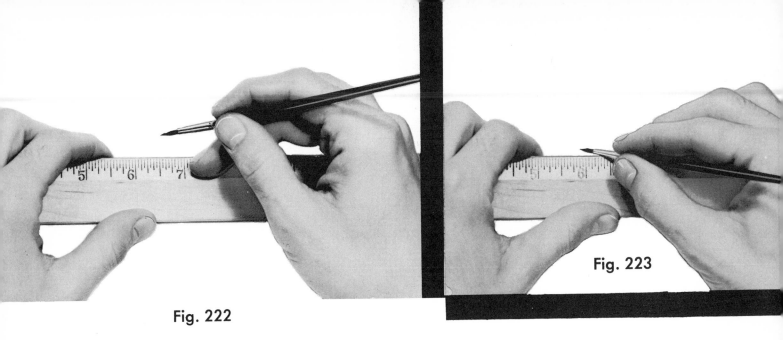

Fig. 222

Fig. 223

FIG. 222. Bring the second finger down so that the fingernail is in contact with the top edge of the ruler and free to slide along this edge. The brush is still held only between the thumb and forefinger.

FIG. 223. Lower the brush so that the metal ferrule of the brush is in contact with the metal edge of the ruler. With the second finger still touching the edge of the ruler, it should be possible to maneuver the brush freely up or down by bending thumb and forefinger.

FIG. 224. The brush is thus placed in contact with the paper, and moved along the ruler to make a straight line. Pressure on the brush should be even, when a line of uniform thickness is desired, as any increased pressure will result in a thicker line.

By starting out with a light pressure, and increasing the pressure as the hand moves along the ruler, a line of varying thickness, from thin to thick, can be obtained. Throughout this procedure, the brush should be almost perpendicular to the paper, and the angle of the brush with the paper should not be changed throughout the stroke. When making lines with pigment, the paint should be just thin enough to flow off the brush, but not so thin that it will spread. It is advisable to practice this thoroughly before trying it on a commercial job.

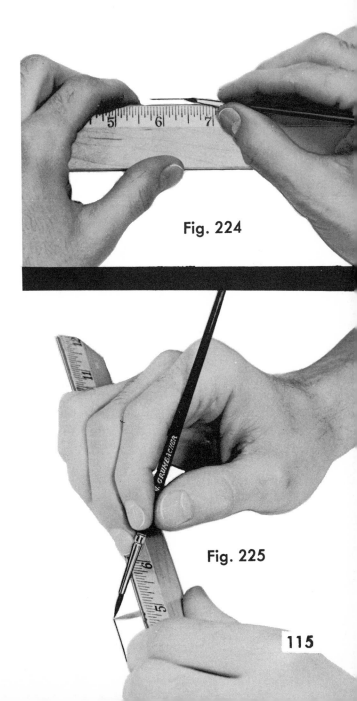

Fig. 224

Fig. 225

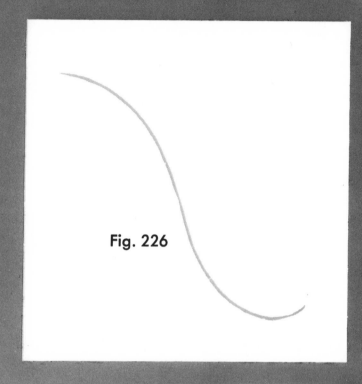

Fig. 226

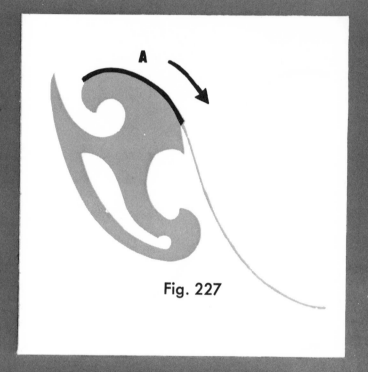

A

Fig. 227

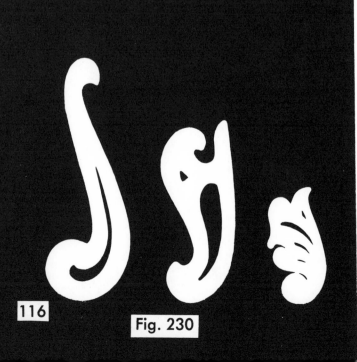

116

Fig. 230

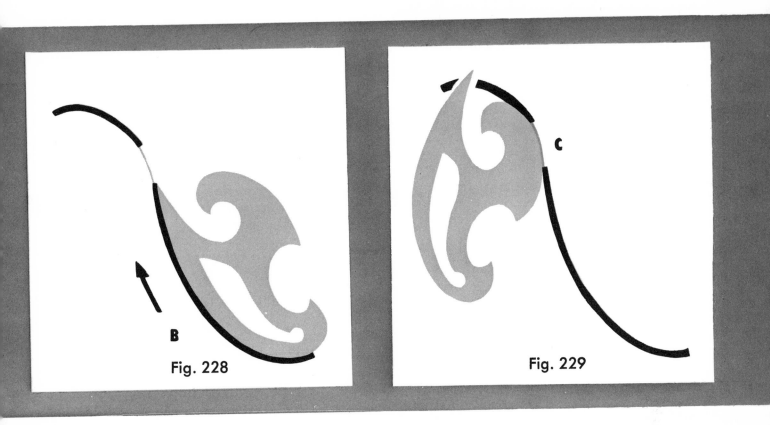

Fig. 228

Fig. 229

Use of the French Curve

FIG. 226. A curved line which is to be drawn accurately and smoothly with the french curve is first sketched lightly in pencil.

FIG. 227. Fit a corresponding section of the french curve to the line at "A" and follow the curve with a pencil.

FIG. 228. Move the french curve to "B" and draw this section of the line.

FIG. 229. Now join "A" and "B" with section "C", completing the drawing of the curved line.

FIG. 230. Curve guides are made in many sizes and shapes to fill various needs. Three irregular curve guides are shown.

Dividing a Line

To divide any straight line into a required number of equal divisions, a simple and accurate method which does not involve the use of mathematics may be applied.

FIG. 231. This line, AB, which is 6½″ long, is to be divided into 7 equal divisions. FIG. 232. From one end (A) of the line, draw another line at an angle of 45 degrees or less: and, of a length almost equal to the line AB. FIG. 233. Starting at point A, mark off seven equal divisions on this line. These can be of any convenient dimension which will not extend beyond the line. In this particular example 1″ divisions are used. FIG. 234. From the last mark on this line extend a line to point B with a triangle. While in this same position set a T-square against the base of the triangle so that parallel lines from each mark can be drawn to the line AB, as shown on page 23. FIG. 235. Three of the lines have been drawn in this manner and a fourth is being completed. It can be seen that we are dividing the original line into the same number of divisions (seven) as marked off on the new line. FIG. 236 shows the entire construction, with the original line divided into seven equal parts. The construction lines are now erased. For clarity the parallel lines were drawn in this procedure, but in practice it is not necessary to actually *draw* the parallel lines, merely mark off the points where they intersect.

A ——————————————————————————— B

Fig. 231

Fig. 232

Fig. 233

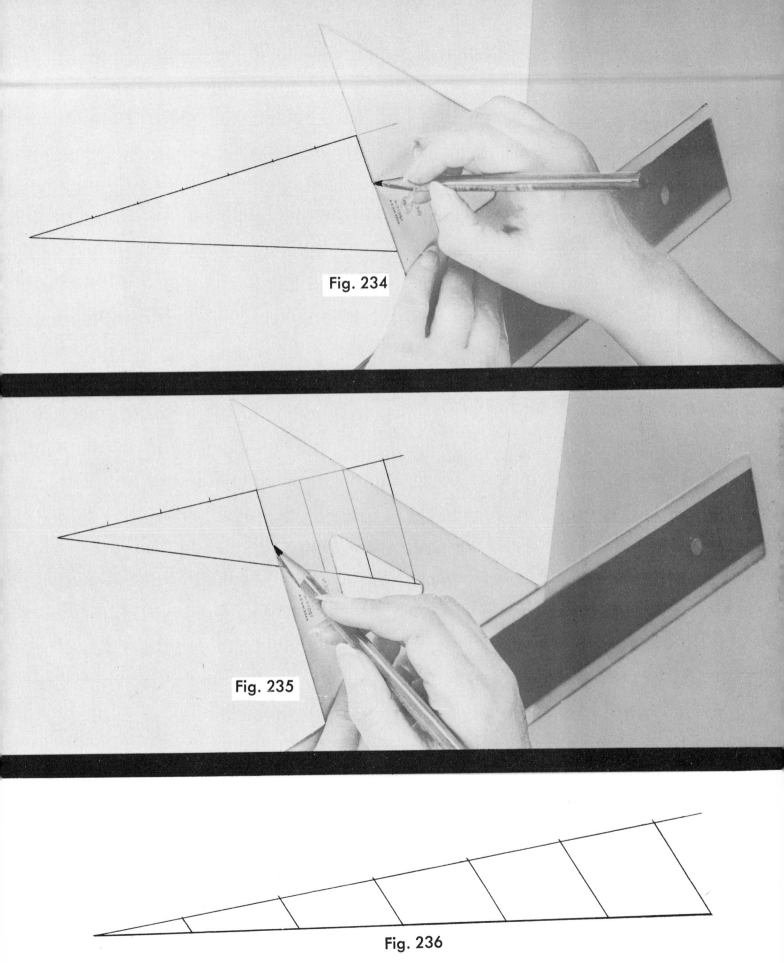

Fig. 234

Fig. 235

Fig. 236

PHOTOGRAPHS
AND PHOTOSTATS

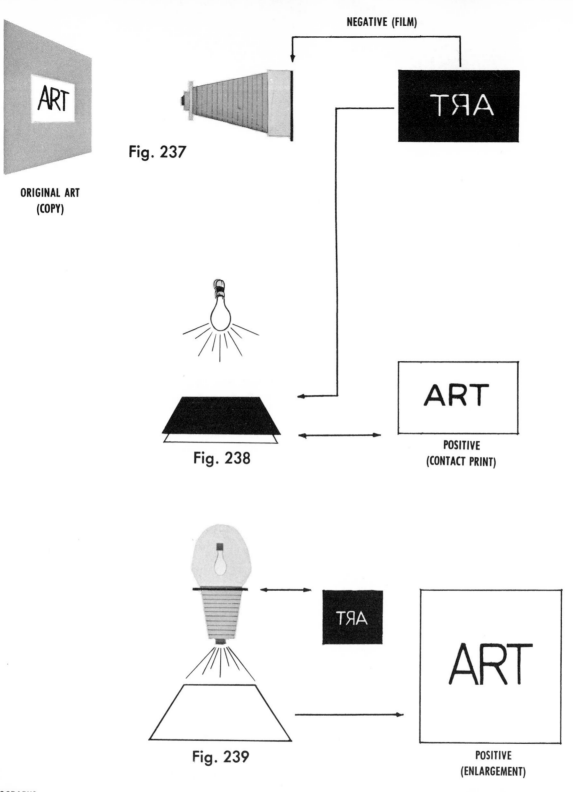

ORIGINAL ART
(COPY)

Fig. 237

NEGATIVE (FILM)

Fig. 238

POSITIVE
(CONTACT PRINT)

Fig. 239

POSITIVE
(ENLARGEMENT)

PHOTOGRAPHS

PHOTOSTATS

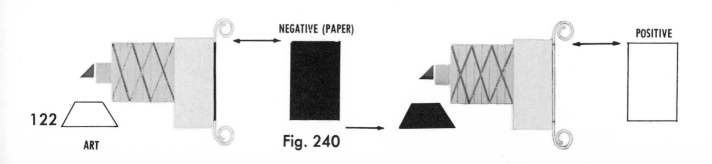

NEGATIVE (PAPER)

POSITIVE

ART

Fig. 240

122

Photographic Procedures

Some understanding of basic photographic procedures is helpful in planning and executing layouts and making use of photographs and photostats in general. Any artwork, or photograph, to be reproduced by printing must first be rephotographed or "copied" by the platemaker.

FIG. 237. The artwork or photograph to be copied is set up before the camera and exposed to film which is developed into a negative of the original art. This negative may be either the same size, smaller, or larger than the original art, depending upon: 1. the size of the original art, 2. the size at which the art is to be reproduced, 3. the camera equipment available. In plate-making the negative is made the same size as the plate image, which would be the same size as the reproduction.

FIG. 238. If this negative is placed in close contact with a sheet of photographic paper, and exposed to light through the negative, a positive image, on the paper (same as the original art) results upon development. This image, naturally, is the same size as the negative image. The negative image may be transferred to metal printing plates instead of photographic paper by the platemaker.

FIG. 239. If a positive image *larger* than the negative is required, the negative is inserted in an enlarger and the image projected onto a sheet of photographic enlarging paper. It can be made any size, if the original negative is sharp.

Making a Photostat

FIG. 240. A photostat differs from a photograph in that the negative image is made on *paper* rather than on film, and that the process is used primarily to duplicate flat, two dimensional images such as drawings, lettering and other photographs, rather than to photograph three-dimensional objects, or persons, as a camera would do. If the original is straight black and white copy the stat will do as well as a photograph; but for halftone images a copy *photograph* gives better tonal value. However, halftone art is photostated for layout, presentation, size changes, etc. where good reproduction quality is not required.

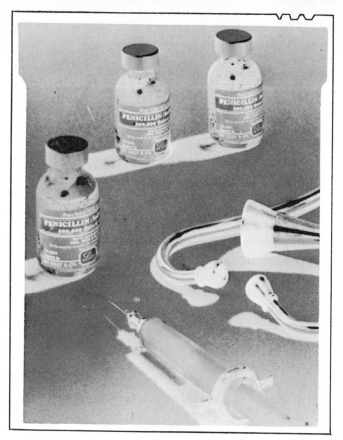

Fig. 241

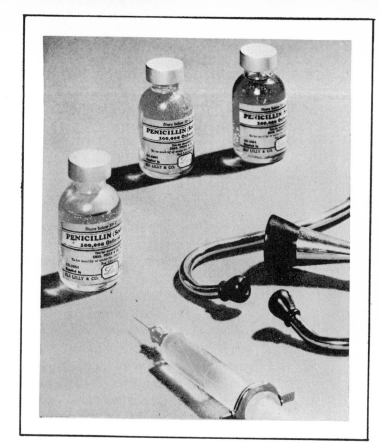

Fig. 242

Photographs

FIG. 241. This is a commercial negative, 3¼″ x 4¼″ in size made on sheet film.

Film is obtainable in roll form, generally used for amateur work; and in sheet form, as shown, generally used for commercial work. The advantage of sheet film is that individual negatives can be exposed and developed as needed, instead of having to wait for a whole roll of film to be exposed before developing. (However, with the 35mm and 2¼″ x 2¼″ reflex cameras being used for commercial work, especially color, roll film is used commercially.)

FIG. 242. This is a contact paper print made from the sheet film, the image being exactly the same size as in the negative.

FIG. 243. This is a photographic paper enlargement of the entire negative. A good sharp negative can be used to make an enlargement, from any size slightly larger than the original negative, to mural size. When the size photograph desired is larger than available size photo paper, the image is distributed over two or more sheets and assembled.

FIG. 244. When a negative is projected in an enlarger the whole negative is simultaneously enlarged. However, it is possible to select only a desired portion of the enlarged image, either by masking the negative so that only the required portion is exposed, or by placing the enlarging paper only under the area of the image selected. This illustration is a selected portion of our original negative, enlarged to required size.

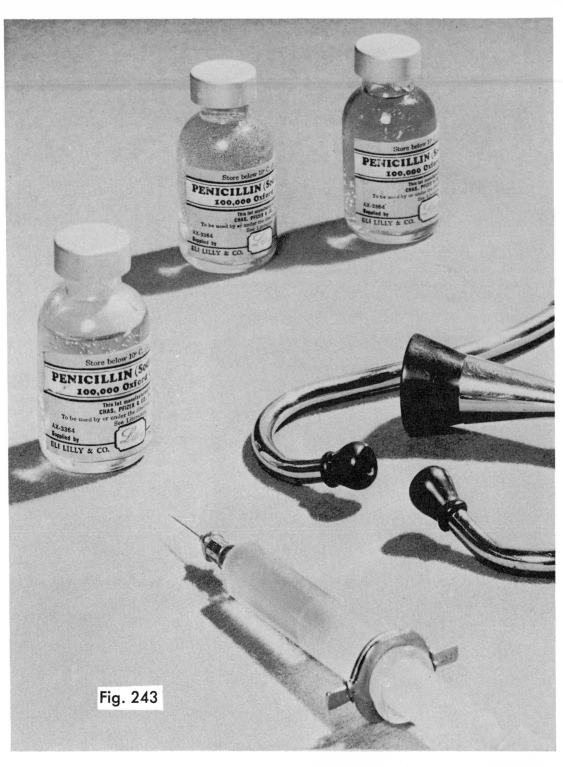

Fig. 243

Fig. 244

Fig. 245

1⅜"

Fig. 249

Fig. 246

Fig. 247

Photostats

FIG. 245. The original artwork to be photostated is, in this case, a line drawing in ink on bristol board. This is known as the "positive" image.

FIG. 246. The first stage in the photostatic process is to make a "negative", on paper from the original art or "copy". This negative can be made larger or smaller than the original positive. From this negative many variations can be made.

FIG. 247. A positive, any size smaller than the negative, down to one half its size. (If a positive still smaller than this is required, another negative is made from this, then the final reduced positive made from it.)

FIG. 248. A positive, consisting of a black image on a gray ground, instead of on white ground, as in the original art. Another variation obtainable from this same negative would be a positive with a gray image, instead of a black image, on a white ground.

Fig. 248

FIG. 249. A positive, larger than the negative, up to twice its size. In addition, in this photostat the image has been "flopped over"; or, to state it more fundamentally, we have obtained a mirror image of the original, which in certain cases is desirable.

Ordering Photostat Prints

It is necessary to give specific and proper directions when ordering photostats, as they can vary considerably in size, tonal quality and finish, from the original copy supplied. *Types of stats:* Photostats may be made on three different types of paper; glossy, semi-matte and matte finish. The glossy prints give a deeper black, greater tonal value range and sharper detail than the others. They are more expensive, however. *Sizes of stats:* Photostats are made in standard sizes 8½″ x 11″, 11″ x 14″, 14″ x 17″, 17″ x 20″, etc., and are priced accordingly. If only a four inch square image is required, it would be charged on an 8½″ x 11″ basis, the minimum size. Several images can thus be ganged up and one stat made, containing all of them, if in the same scale. In other words, if three small illustrations are pasted on a board, only one stat need be ordered *if they are all required at the same enlargement or reduction.* It is not advisable to put halftone and line art together for stats, if quality reproduction is required in both. Most photostat cameras can only reduce to one-half or enlarge to twice the size of the original, in *one* step. This means that a three inch image can be reduced any size down to one and one-half inches, or enlarged any size up to six inches, from positive to negative; and again reduced one-half or enlarged twice the size from this negative to the positive stage. If still greater positive enlargement or reduction is desired it is necessary to go through still another negative and positive stage. One must keep in mind also that with each stage a certain amount of detail or quality is lost if the artwork is very fine or of subtle tone quality.

Effects and services obtainable: Tonal values of the original art may be modified by means of stats. For example, a dark pencil indication of lettering, or illustration, on tracing paper, which has a gray cast, may be made into a stat of black lettering on a white background if this effect is required. Or suppose that line artwork of several images are pasted up together — a stat of this can be obtained with the pasteup marks eliminated. This also applies to copy which may have soil marks or light discolorations. Just as prints can be made more contrasty than the original art so can they be made "softer" in tonal values. For instance, black lettering on a white background, can become dark gray lettering on a light gray background, or on a white background. The reverse, or mirror image, of an illustration or artwork may be obtained by photostating. Thus a right hand holding a pencil can be converted into a left hand, or the direction of an object reversed. This procedure is called "flopping". Negative images on paper (which we ordinarily see only on film negatives) can be more interesting and effective than the original positive. Comparatively flat three-dimensional objects such as jewelry, drawing instruments, fabrics, etc. can be photostated. This does not provide as good an image as a photograph, but in many instances the effect may be better for a specific purpose. When ordering a photostat be certain to include the following information on the face of the artwork, or, if this is impractical, on a slip of paper attached to it:

1: Whether a positive or negative image is required.
2. The specific size, dimensioned as shown.
3. Type of finish — glossy, semi-matte or matte.
4. Tone effect required (unless obvious from the copy) such as "Sharp black and white," or "Hold halftones as accurately as possible".
5. Your name and address.
6. When wanted — if possible.

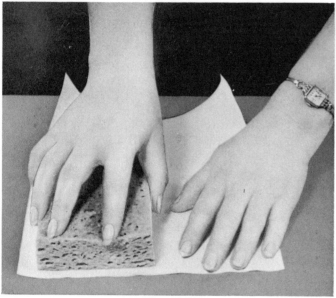

Fig. 250

Mounting Photo Prints

It is often necessary to mount photographs on heavier paper or board for protection, for display or for layout purposes. Most commercially used photographs are single weight, and are therefore comparatively fragile and curl readily. Before using photographs in such condition it is advisable to straighten them out.

FIG. 250. Two single weight, 8″ x 10″ photographs, which have curled.

FIG. 251. Lay the photographs face down, one at a time, on a clean sheet of paper or board, and with a wet sponge dampen the back of the prints evenly.

FIG. 252. Place the prints between lintless blotters, two prints, *face to face;* use as many layers of prints and blotters as necessary or convenient.

FIG. 253. Place several heavy books on this and allow to remain until the prints are dry.

After the prints are dry they may be mounted with rubber cement, as previously explained. If the photographs are to be displayed for a long time, or exposed to strong sunlight the rubber cement will become somewhat brittle and cause peeling, or may stain the photographs. For more permanence photographs are better mounted by use of dry mounting sheets made for this purpose, and used with an electric iron, or preferably with a dry mounting press made for this purpose. A water soluble photopaste is also available, and provides satisfactory mounting.

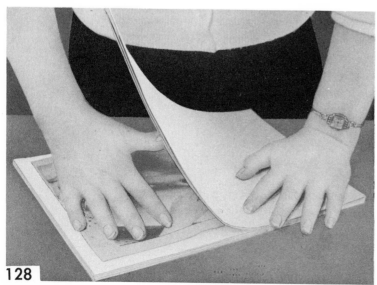

Fig. 251

Fig. 252

Fig. 253

Photo Retouching

Though the artist doing pasteups and mechanicals is not required to do photo retouching, it is helpful to be able to make minor corrections on prints, and he will undoubtedly handle retouched prints. Most retouching on photographs is done with an airbrush, using opaque water color, known as retouch grays. The airbrush is a precise and highly controllable paint sprayer. Linework and simple flat tone retouching are done with the ordinary sable brush. (See next page.) Linework can also be done with the ruling pen, using retouch grays, lampblack or poster white. Correcting minor defects in a print, such as black or white spots, hairlines, etc., is known as "spotting". This is done with the sablebrush, using opaque water color for lightening and either opaque water color or transparent dye for darkening. It is also possible to etch out dark lines or spots with a sharp blade.

Before retouching a print it should be mounted on mat board, or temporarily adhered to it with masking tape. The print is then rubbed down with talcum powder or fine pumice applied with absorbent cotton to provide a better base for the paint. The hand should not be placed directly on the photograph after this cleaning operation as paint will not adhere on greasy areas. Keep a piece of scrap paper beneath the hand for this purpose. When paint does not adhere to a surface, whether it be a photograph, acetate or paper, a wetting or adhering agent can be used in the paint. These are obtainable at art stores under various trade names.

Spotting Prints

Slight defects in photographic prints can be corrected and minor alterations made by any art-trained person. Most artists do not realize that it is quite feasible to use pencil, opaque watercolor and transparent dye on a photograph or photostat. Pencil or diluted black dye can be used to darken a light area or line; opaque watercolor can be used to lighten an area or line.

Pencil takes best on a semi-matte or matte print, though a very soft pencil (4B) sharply pointed, can be used even on a glossy print to darken or obliterate little white specks, or hold an edge or outline on an object. Never press hard with the pencil, and be careful not to rub the spot off accidentally, once applied. On a matte print the pencil tone can be rubbed in with a stomp to give an even tone to a spot or area.

Black or white poster color, or a mixture of both to provide various tints of gray, can be used to lighten or darken a spot or area to be changed. The paint should be thick enough to remain opaque, otherwise it will not cover, and will take unevenly. Opaque watercolor can be removed from the print as shown on page 133.

Diluted india ink, or retouching dye can only be used to darken an area, especially where a certain degree of transparency is required. Dye adheres well to a glossy print, but it should be applied diluted and the tone built up gradually, as it cannot be removed.

A photographic dye known as "Spotone" is sold in kit form, in various gray tones, both warm and cool, since most prints have either a slightly brownish or bluish cast.

Fig. 254

Fig. 255

FIG. 254. A glossy print with a fairly large white imperfection on the racket and two small black specks on the center tennis ball, which have been circled with a black grease or china marking pencil for identification. (This is a practical method of marking prints as the grease pencil does not indent the photo, and it can easily be rubbed off completely with a piece of cotton.)

FIG. 255. If this were a matte or semi-matte print the white spot could be carefully pencilled in as shown. However, since it is glossy, it should be darkened either with Spotone or with black and white poster color mixed to match the background color perfectly. Do not judge the gray tone when wet. Apply it to the spot and allow it to dry, then decide whether it should be made lighter or darker to match. The test spot can be removed with slightly wet cotton.

Fig. 256   **Fig. 257**

FIG. 256. The dark specks on the tennis ball could also be corrected in the same manner, or they might, as shown, be removed by gently etching away the surface of the photo with a sharp knife or razor blade.

FIG. 257. The print, after the light and dark spots have been corrected. Now we shall lighten the racket strings in the upper area of the racket, so that they will show up better in reproduction, FIG. 258.

FIG. 259. They are merely drawn over the opaque white poster color, applied carefully with a good, pointed red sable brush. Paint or ink can also be applied to a photo with a ruling pen, but in this case it would have appeared too mechanical. Compare this photograph with the one directly above for effect.

Fig. 258   **Fig. 259**

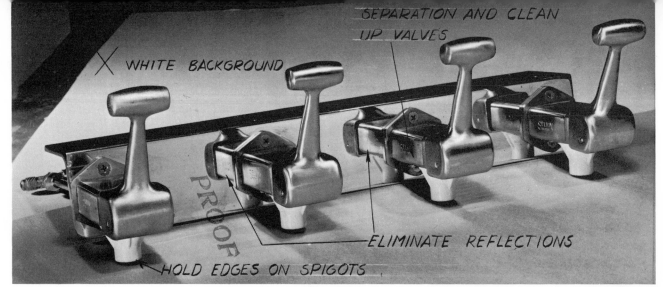

Fig. 260

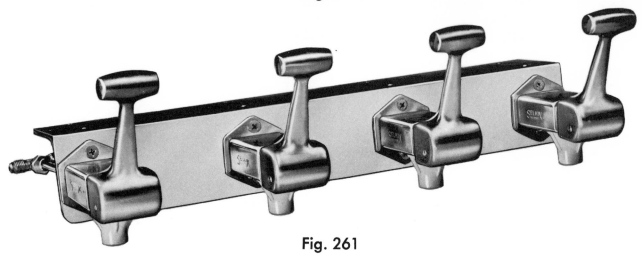

Fig. 261

Photo Retouching

A typical "retouch" job is shown before and after the "cleaning up" operation. Directions provided by the client are shown written on a *spare* print, FIG. 260, which was given the artist with a duplicate print to be retouched. Aside from airbrushing a white background and removing reflections from the bracket, some shadows and highlights are added to the spigots and a little linework added to hold the edges, FIG. 261. Instead of airbrushing the background, it might have been prepared for silhouetting by a white brush line as indicated on page 67.

Airbrushing a Background

It is not intended to provide instruction in airbrushing in this book, as it is not within its scope. However, an acquaintance with the technique is advisable, and if more information is needed the reader can find it in books written specifically on this subject, including this author's "Complete Airbrush Book".

As an example of a typical airbrush retouch operation let us consider a simple background job, FIG. 262. The dispenser does not stand out well against the dark background area, so the background must be lightened to correct this defect. FIG. 263. Either opaque white, or light retouch-gray watercolor is evenly airbrushed over the entire photograph, but not applied too heavily. At this stage it is semi-transparent, and the image can still be seen through the paint. FIG. 264. With a piece of moistened cotton wrapped around the end of a brush, carefully wipe the paint away from the areas where it is not wanted. The swab should be turned after each stroke, and replaced after a few strokes. Compare FIGS. 262 and 265 for the effect of this simple operation. This retouching could also have been done by adhering a piece of frisket paper to the photograph with rubber cement, then carefully cutting it with a sharp

Fig. 262

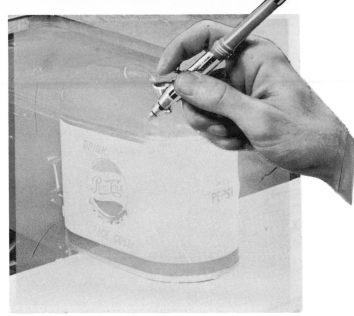

Fig. 263

Fig. 264

Fig. 265

razor blade or frisket knife along the outline of the dispenser, and removing the frisket paper from the background only. Thus the area where the paint is not required will be protected during airbrushing. The frisket paper is removed after sufficient paint has been applied to the background, and it will not be necessary to wipe away paint.

Making a Swab

FIG. 266. Shave the paint from the handle end of a thin paintbrush. Flatten out a small wad of cotton, and place the brush end in its center. Twirl the cotton firmly around the brush end, tapering the cotton at the bottom rather tightly.

 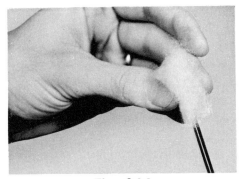 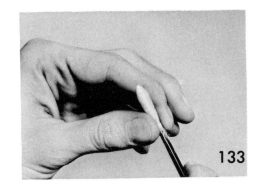

Fig. 266

REPRODUCTION

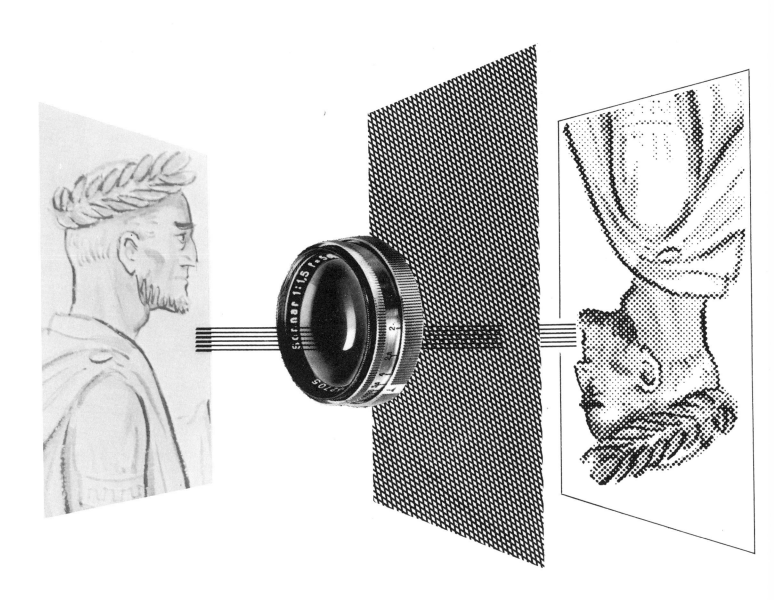

Fig. 268

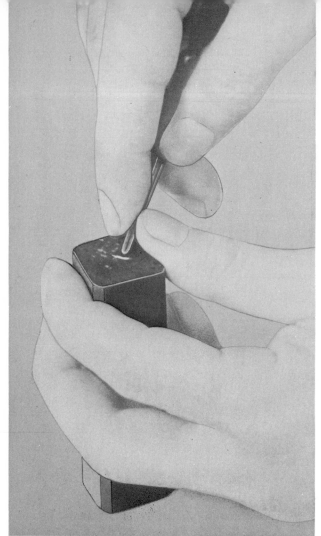

Fig. 267

Basic Principles

Some knowledge of the basic principle of printing is helpful for an understanding of production procedures, and especially for the preparation of mechanicals and pre-separated art for color printing.

FIG. 267. If small lines or areas are gouged out of the end of a block of wood and—

FIG. 268, this end pressed firmly on a black inkpad; then—

FIG. 269, pressed on a sheet of white paper—

FIG. 270, an imprint will result, which is black where the wood was left standing and white where the lines and area were gouged out.

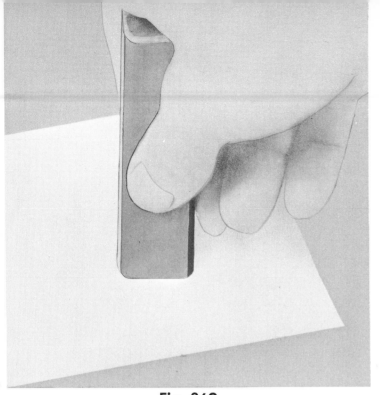

Fig. 269

Fig. 270

Fig. 271

Fig. 272

FIG. 271. Since any number of duplicate impressions could be obtained by this method, we can consider this a form of printing. In principle, such a procedure was used for a long time, and still is, in the form of wood cuts and wood engravings.

FIG. 272. If, instead of using a black ink, gray or any other color ink were used, the same cut block would give the same impression in this color.

FIG. 273. If we wish to combine another image in black with the previous image in gray, we merely print the gray image first, then, FIG. 274, the black image over it for this combined "two color" effect.

In current practice, metal plates are used instead of wood and the image transferred photographically and etched out with acid. In letterpress printing the image or printing surface is in relief, in gravure it is recessed, and in lithography a flat photographic image of water repellent characteristic is utilized. This, of course is a very generalized and simplified description.

Fig. 273

Fig. 274

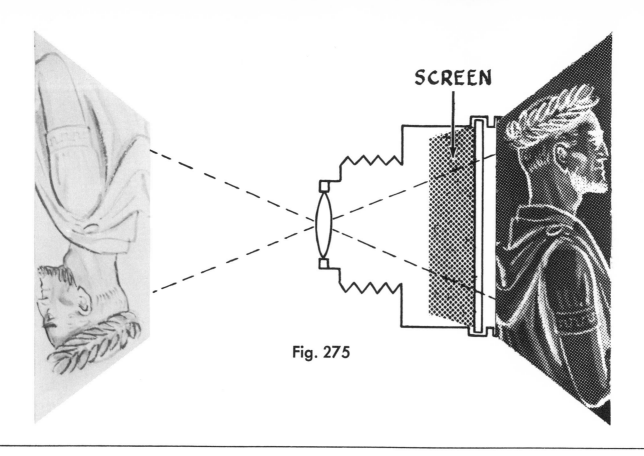

Fig. 275

Artwork of any kind may be classified in two categories, insofar as printing is concerned: *line art,* and *halftone* art. This applies to color as well as black and white. Line art is that which consists strictly of black and white images, with no intermediary gray tones. An illusion of gray tones may be present, but if this is the result of fine black dots or lines, it is still line art. Solid black ink, for instance, no matter how used—drybrush, stipple, etc., is still only line art; but, if the ink is diluted with water, it immediately becomes halftone art. Lead pencil, gray pastel, a mixture of black and white poster color—all of these result in artwork that is in the halftone category. Line art is photographed directly onto a negative, from which a printing plate is made; but halftone art necessitates the use of screens in conjunction with the negative.

Halftone screens are made with different size lines, some screens having only 45 lines to the inch, others as many as 160 lines to the inch. The finer the screen the more faithful the reproduction is to the original, if printed properly. Newspapers, because of the manner in which they are printed on poor quality paper, require coarse screen plates. On good coated stock, fine screen plates can be used.

Photoengraving

Briefly and schematically, the process of making a relief printing plate (used in letterpress) from halftone artwork, is as illustrated.

FIG. 275. The artwork is set up in front of the camera, which has a glass screen between the lens and the negative, close to the negative, but not in direct contact. The image passes through this screen and is broken up into vari-sized and spaced dots which affect the photographic emulsion on the negative film. The developed negative appears as in the illustration.

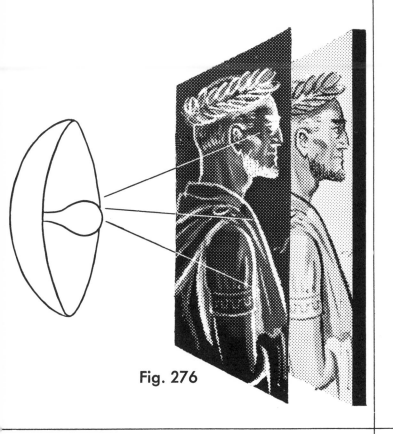

Fig. 276

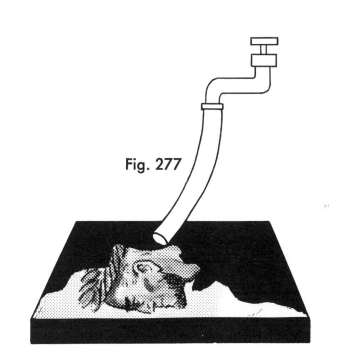

Fig. 277

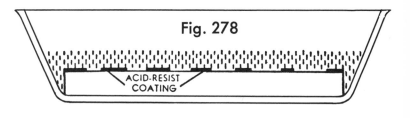

Fig. 278

ACID-RESIST COATING

Fig. 279

FIG. 276. The negative is placed in direct contact with a metal plate (zinc or copper) which has its surface coated with a photographic sensitizer. This is exposed to a strong light. The light passes only through the clear portions of the negative, which represent the tones in the original artwork.

FIG. 277. The plate is washed with water. Where the light passes through the clear areas of the negative the sensitizer on the plate hardens and becomes insoluble in water. The remaining areas therefore wash off, leaving the plate coated with an image of the artwork, in vari-size dot formation.

FIG. 278. The plate is exposed to acid, which eats away the metal where there is no image (no coating to protect it).

FIG. 279. When these areas are sufficiently etched away they form a relief plate like the woodcut, the top surfaces making up the image.

FIG. 280. This shows the relief plate with its dots forming an image which can be inked and printed. The insert shows a portion magnified.

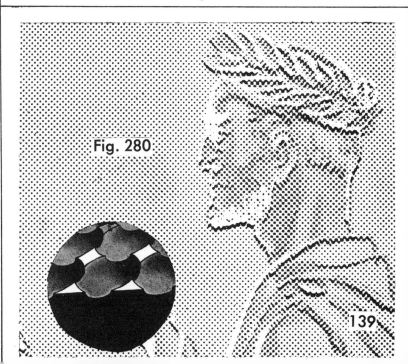

Fig. 280

139

Fig. 281

Veloxes

If a photo-paper contact print is made from the screened negative, it is called a Velox. Veloxes usually are ordered from halftone art because, once having been screened it becomes line art and can be pasted up with other line art such as line drawings, lettering, or photostats, and a line plate made. The cost of producing the printing plate by this method is very considerably reduced.

FIG. 281. Assume that we are to have this halftone art reproduced. When ordering a halftone printing plate it is necessary to specify the kind of plate required, as different types are available. The simplest and least expensive of the halftone plates is the *square halftone,* FIG. 282. Compare this with the "original art", and you will note that there are no white areas and no solid black lines. The screen has caused this. It is possible to obtain a *highlight halftone,* FIG. 283, wherein the highlights and white are retained; or for still greater fidelity, a *combination plate,* FIG. 284, wherein both highlights and line are held. These effects

Fig. 282

Fig. 283

Fig. 284

can also be secured by retouching a velox with black or white paint, thus obtaining a combination plate for slightly more than the cost of a square halftone, FIGS. 286 and 287. Images of various sizes can be made as veloxes from the original halftone and be pasted up with type for different size ads, labels, packages, etc.

FIG. 285. This portion of the velox was considerably enlarged to show the dot pattern of a coarse screen print. Compare this with the fine screen print, FIG. 284.

Fig. 285

Fig. 286

Fig. 287

141

Fig. 288

Type

FIG. 288. You are undoubtedly familiar with nameplates printed from hand stamps made up of individual rubber letters, assembled to form the name. This is actually a relief (letterpress) form of printing, like the woodcut previously described; but now limited to letter forms. You will also note in the illustration that the letters are in reverse (mirror image) in the stamp, so that, when inked and printed, the letters read correctly. Basically, type is made up of the same individual letter forms, but made of metal in most cases. Type *may* be assembled by hand for composition, but usually this is done mechanically. The illustration, FIG. 289, on this page shows an assemblage of varied size and form letters locked together in preparation for printing.

Fig. 289

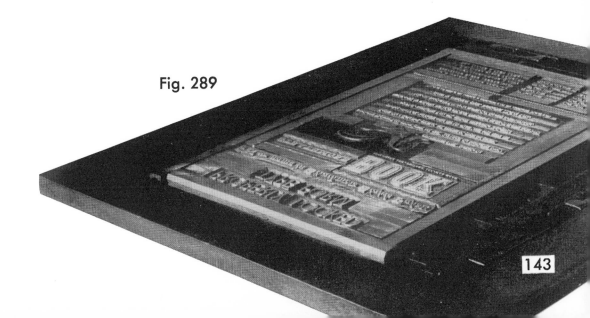

COLOR

SEPARATIONS

Fig. 290

Color Separation Mechanical

A considerable amount of artwork made up of flat color (line plates) is prepared as "pre-separated" art. Just as each color is printed from a separate plate, so the artwork is thus prepared on correspondingly separate sheets of paper or acetate overlays. The art is drawn in black ink, regardless of the final colors in which the design is to be printed. It is simpler and much less expensive to photograph the artwork in this form for platemaking. Each printing plate is then inked in the color corresponding to that indicated by the artist in the original and each color plate in sequence, in register with the previous colors. Let's examine a simple trademark to be printed in two flat colors, that is, from "line" plates.

Fig. 291

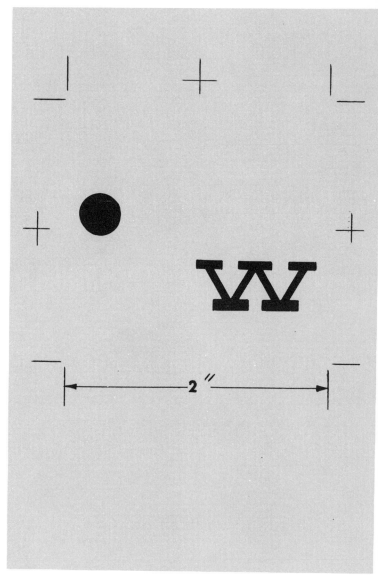

Fig. 292

The mechanical is prepared as follows:

FIG. 290. A rough sketch of the trademark design, the background to be printed blue, the dot of the "I" and the "W" to be printed in red. The "I" and the "P" will remain the color of the paper, in this case, white.

FIG. 291. A drawing on white illustration board is made in black ink, representing only the blue area to be printed. This is done same size as the finish will be. It is marked for size as indicated, and three registration marks (I) placed close to the artwork, one above and one on each side. This will enable us to register the drawing for the second color with this first color, even though it will be on a separate sheet.

FIG. 292. An acetate or tracing paper overlay is taped over this drawing for the second color, and the registration marks immediately and accurately copied. (Printed registration marks on clear Scotch tape are available.) While thus in register the drawing is made of the "dot" and the "W" in black, on the overlay, allowing a very slight overlap of the two colors.

FIG. 293. The acetate overlay is shown slightly lifted from the base drawing underneath.

FIG. 294. A plate is made from FIG. 291 and printed in blue (represented here by gray) on white paper; then, on this, the plate from FIG. 292 is printed in red (black here) for the final result.

If this were to have been a cut-out label, with the color printed right to the edge (bleeding) of the cut-out, the drawings would have been made ¼" larger all around as shown on page 149, FIG. 296, and the excess trimmed off after printing. This same situation occurred in the printing of the composite in one color, pages 76 and 77.

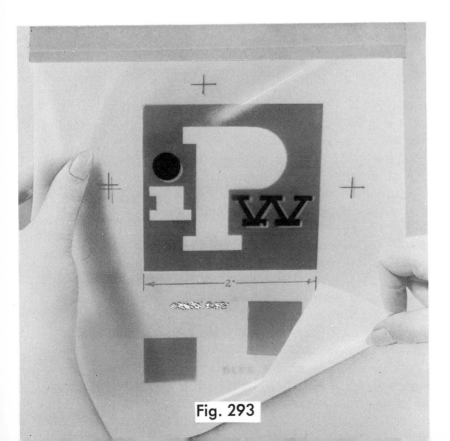

Fig. 293

Fig. 294

147

Fig. 295

Two-Color Mechanical (Line Art)

The original throw-away reproduced on next page was printed in two colors, red and blue. Since this book is only printed in black ink, we are indicating the blue by a gray tone in this reproduction, FIG. 298, and the black represents the red tone. In so-called pre-separated color artwork, the artist prepares all artwork in black if it is line copy, and generally prepares the artwork representing each different color on a separate sheet of paper or overlay.

FIG. 295 is the complete mechanical prepared to reproduce the two color card, shown in FIG. 298. FIG. 296. On the opposite page, you will note that the overlay, now separated from the mechanical, contains only the artwork which is shown as black (red in the original) in FIG. 298. Note the registration marks, circles with crosses, on each side of the artwork, and the trim marks indicating the bleed to be trimmed off after the card is printed. FIG. 297, shows artwork on the key drawing of the mechanical which is represented by gray tones (blue in the original) in FIG. 298.

It also has registration marks and crop marks which are in exactly the same relative position as the art for the red plate. A line cut (printing plate) is made from each mechanical, the former inked with red ink and printed, the latter inked with blue ink and printed, in register with the previous one. The artwork on the opposite page was intentionally photographed so that the actual cut-outs would show. Also note that in the dark rectangular block with reverse lettering, the area on which the lettering is located is jet black, whereas the area surrounding this is a very dark gray. This is due to the fact that the lettering was on a black glossy stat whereas, in the area surrounding, it was inked in with black ink which was not quite as dark as the stat. However, they are both black and therefore, printed as a solid in the reproduction, with no difference in tonal value between the two areas. Note also that since the red arrow is projected into the block represented by the blue plate, the area of overlap was left white on the blue plate. If this had not been done, the red arrow printing on the blue background would have given either a very dark, or a purple impression, as shown by the dark line on the right hand side of the arrow head in FIG. 298, where a slight overlap of the two colors occurred.

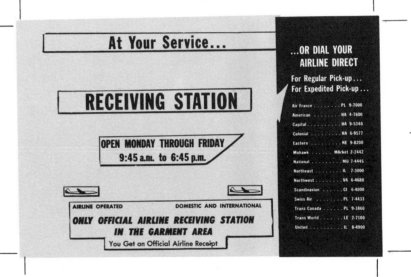

Fig. 296

Fig. 297

Fig. 298

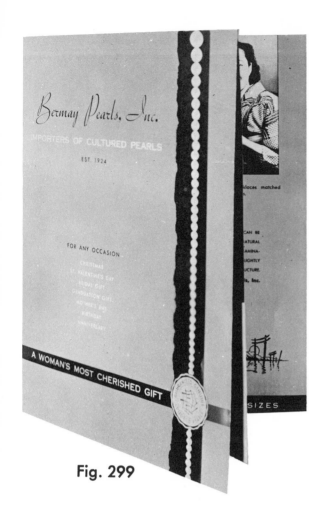

Fig. 299

Mechanical Halftone and Solid, French-Fold

FIG. 299. This is a french-fold brochure, printed in two colors; a halftone black (which of course includes the solid black) represented by the lettering and photographs, and a solid pink (shown here in flat gray) representing the background. These are more clearly shown in the inside of the open brochure, FIG. 300. (See page 138 for explanation of halftone and line art.) Referring to the top illustration again, it will be noted that the fold occurs along the top edge, as well as the back edge. Actually, this brochure consists of only one sheet of paper, folded in this manner, and necessitating careful consideration of the layout of the artwork on the mechanical, FIG. 301, so that everything is in proper reading position when printed and folded.

This mechanical represents only the black plate (halftone and solid). The pink plate is represented by an acetate overlay, not shown here, with solid black wherever the background pink occurs. In order to make clear the actual units of pasteup for clarity of instruction here, the background color of the mechanical illustrated is shown with a light gray tone, although it is really white illustration board. The two blank areas represent the position of photographs that are larger than they will appear on this brochure, therefore must be reduced when being copied, and stripped in on the negative of the complete mechanical.

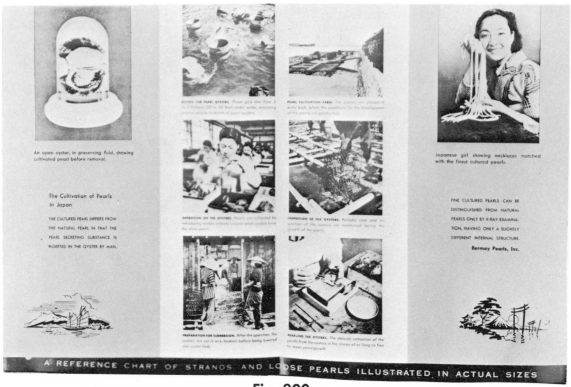

Fig. 300

A WOMAN'S MOST CHERISHED GIFT

FOR ANY OCCASION

CHRISTMAS
ST. VALENTINE'S DAY
BRIDAL GIFT
GRADUATION GIFT
MOTHER'S DAY
BIRTHDAY
ANNIVERSARY

IMPORTERS OF CULTURED PEARLS

Bernay Pearls, Inc.

EST. 1924

THIS IS A USEFUL GUIDE FOR SELLING
AND ORDERING CULTURED PEARLS

You will find this folder unusually helpful and interesting in its illustration and description of actual sizes of necklaces and individual cultured pearls. This folder and the accompanying Order Book will facilitate the selection and ordering of our cultured pearls.

Bernay Pearls, Inc.

An open oyster, in preserving fluid, showing cultivated pearl before removal.

THE CULTURED PEARL DIFFERS FROM THE NATURAL PEARL IN THAT THE PEARL SECRETING SUBSTANCE IS INSERTED IN THE OYSTER BY MAN.

DIVING FOR PEARL OYSTERS. These girls dive from 5 to 7 fathoms (30 to 42 feet) under water, remaining several minutes in search of pearl oysters.

OPERATION ON THE OYSTERS. Pearls are cultivated by introducing nucleus irritants around which oysters form the shiny pearls.

PREPARATION FOR SUBMERSION. After the operation, the oysters are put in wire baskets before being lowered into oyster beds.

PEARL CULTIVATION FARM. The oysters are placed in water beds, where the conditions for the development of the pearls is satisfactory.

INSPECTION OF THE OYSTERS. Periodic care and inspection of the oysters is maintained during the growth of the pearls.

PEARLING THE OYSTERS. The delicate extraction of the pearls from the oysters is the climax of as long as five to seven years growth.

Japanese girl showing necklaces matched with the finest cultured pearls.

FINE CULTURED PEARLS CAN BE DISTINGUISHED FROM NATURAL PEARLS ONLY BY X-RAY EXAMINATION, HAVING ONLY A SLIGHTLY DIFFERENT INTERNAL STRUCTURE.

Fig. 301

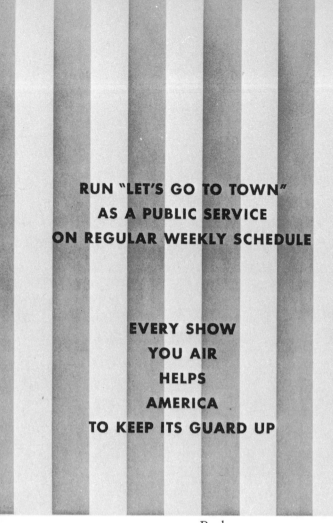

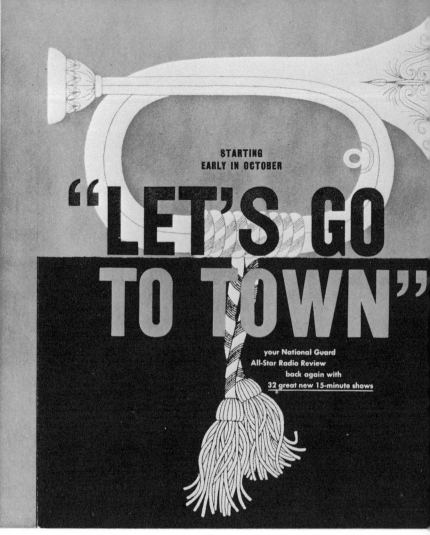

Back   FIG. 303.   Front

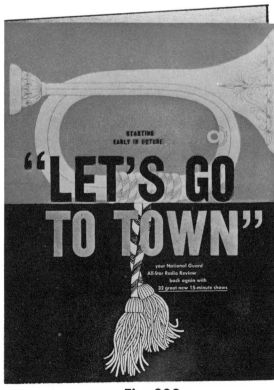

Fig. 302

FIG. 302. A brochure printed in two colors, blue halftone, and solid red. The dark tones, including the photographs, represent the blue impression. The mechanicals are shown on the following pages.

THIS YEAR

"Let's Go To Town" features Great Bands and Singers Like These . . .

BANDS ★ RAY ANTHONY ★ RALPH FLANAGAN ★

RALPH MARTERIE ★ THE FABULOUS DORSEYS ★ BILLY MAY ★

HARRY JAMES ★ LES BAXTER ★ LES BROWN ★

RICHARD MALTBY ★ HAL McINTYRE

VOCALISTS ★ PATTI PAGE ★ MINDY CARSON ★

PEGGY LEE ★ JONI JAMES ★ GEORGIA GIBBS ★

KITTY KALLEN ★ THERESA BREWER ★

LILLIAN BRIGGS ★ LES PAUL & MARY FORD ★ JUNE VALLI

Patti Page

Mindy Carson

Peggy Lee

Joni James

Georgia Gibbs

Kitty Kallen

Lillian Briggs

Les Paul & Mary Ford

June Valli

FIG. 304. Inside double page spread

FIG. 305. Cover mechanical, red plate
on illustration board

FIG. 306. Cover mechanical, blue plate, tracing paper overlay

FIG. 307. Overlay of red plate mechanical placed in position, with blue plate mechanical underneath.

FIG. 308. Both mechanicals in position, the red plate overlay of tracing paper on top, and the blue plate mechanical showing through lightly.

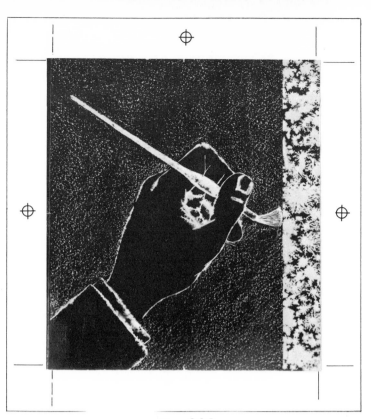

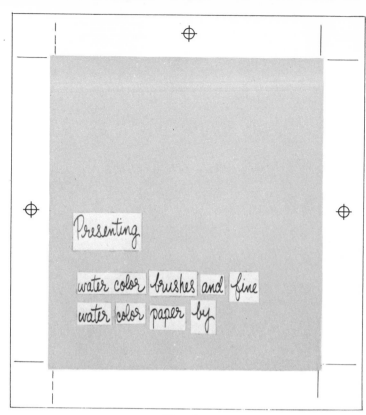

Fig. 309   **Fig. 310**

Mechanical Special Effects

In this instance a mechanical for a brochure is prepared for a two color separation, one of which is a halftone color (black), and the other a solid color (red). The particular mechanical shown here involves the use of a pen and ink illustration, negative photostats, photographs, hand lettering, pasteup lettering and type proofs. This is not a commercial job, but an assignment prepared by a student in the author's class in production procedures.

FIG. 309. The mechanical for the black plate of the cover. The drawing of the hand was done in black ink on dampened rough watercolor paper. After the paper dried the "dot" or stipple effect was achieved by going over the surface lightly with a black grease pencil, which marked only the raised surfaces of the paper. The effect on the right hand border was achieved by dropping india ink of the wet paper in various spots and letting it run slightly. This was cut out and pasted in position with the first drawing, then a negative photostat made of this combination. This gave a reversal of value, as seen here, which provides an interesting effect. Note that the artwork was made larger to allow for trimming off, after printing, the areas which "bleed." Since the back of this cover is plain white it is not shown here in order to save space. However, in the actual mechanical it would be shown, in outline, to the left of the dotted line fold marks.

FIG. 310. Instead of doing the hand lettering in white directly on the black background, an overlay of tracing paper was prepared in register with the black plate, and the hand lettering pasted on it as shown. Each word is on a separate piece of paper because some words were re-lettered until properly drawn. The fact that the tracing paper is gray and the lettering is on white paper does not matter because this will be photographed as line copy and the light tone will not affect the negative. The lettering will be "dropped out" (or reversed) on the black plate, so that the *lettering itself* will not print, only the area around it, giving the effect of white lettering.

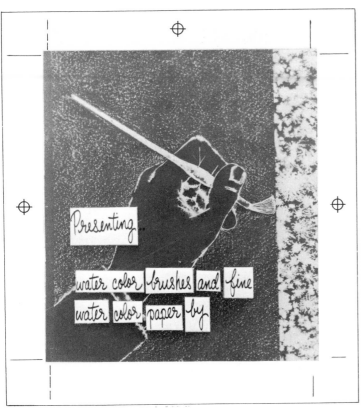

Fig. 311

Fig. 312

FIG. 311. The tracing overlay, with the lettering, is shown in register with the black plate drawing.

FIG. 312. The pasteup of lettering for the red plate. "Winsor & Newton" is a type proof; the rest is acetate pasteup lettering; the trademark is a photostat of the original drawing.

FIG. 313 shows the finished reproduction of the cover of the brochure. The gray tones represent the artwork printed in red in the actual brochure.

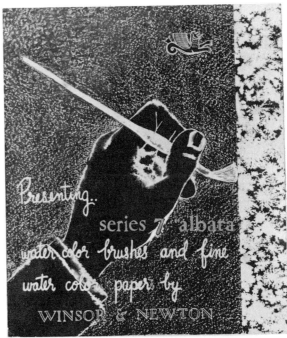

Fig. 313

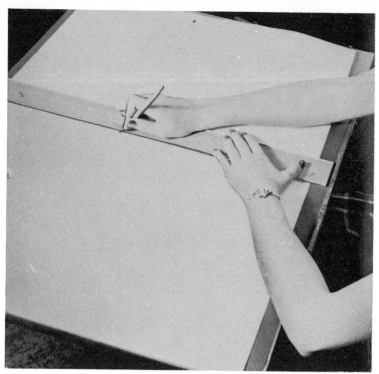

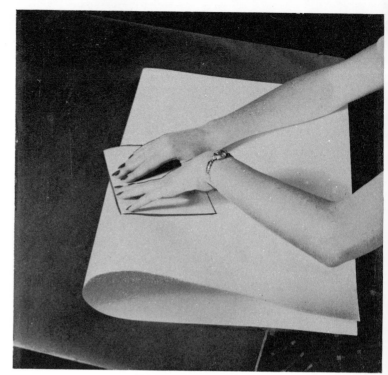

Fig. 314   Fig. 315

Protecting Pasteups and Mechanicals

For protection in handling, and for more effective presentation, artwork should be matted and flapped if it is on a board, or mounted if it is on lightweight paper. A simple method which combines mounting and matting in one operation is shown here, for application to artwork done on a comparatively thin or lightweight stock.

FIG. 314. Select a large sheet of medium or heavyweight paper at least twice the size of the drawing (including border) to be matted. Score a straight line down the center of the paper by cutting very lightly into it with a razor blade.

FIG. 315. Turn the paper over and fold it along the scored line which should be on the *outside* of the fold. Note that a piece of scrap paper is held under the hand so as not to soil the mat.

FIG. 316. Rule in an area the same size as the artwork which is to show, allowing a slightly wider border on the bottom than on the top and sides. This is done on the front sheet of the mat.

FIG. 317. Cut this section out of the front sheet and remove it.

FIG. 318. Open the mat and secure the artwork with scotch tape or rubber cement to the inside face of the back of the mat. Be certain that it centered properly.

FIG. 319. Fold over the front flap, and the matting is complete. The mat can be made in such manner as to fold on the top instead of the side, if desired. A sheet of clear acetate can be placed over the drawing, underneath the front mat.

Fig. 316   Fig. 317

Fig. 318   Fig. 319

Mechanicals are generally done on illustration board. Since the borders of the artwork usually carry notations for the production artist and engraver or lithographer, as well as the printer, it is not feasible to mat the work. The whole front of the illustration board, however, is covered with a sheet of tracing paper, for protection.

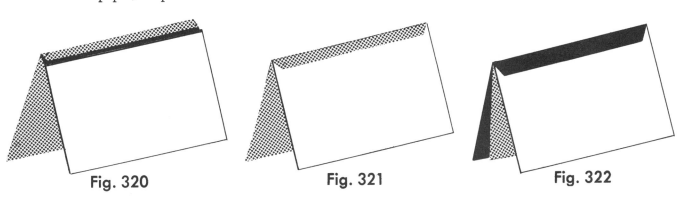

Fig. 320   Fig. 321   Fig. 322

FIG. 320. Assuming that we are looking at the back of the illustration board upon which the mechanical has been made, this shows a sheet of tracing paper, folded along its top edge, ready to be adhered to the top back edge of the illustration board with rubber cement.

FIG. 321. The flap is now adhered and the corners trimmed off for neatness.

FIG. 322. Over the tracing paper another flap may now be added, this one of kraft paper, or heavy wrapping or colored drawing paper, to provide added protection, and a presentable cover.

GLOSSARY

BLEED

The term used to denote printing or art work which is carried to the edge of the page. In the original art this must be carried beyond the line which indicates the edge of the printed page.

BROCHURE

A small advertising booklet.

CALL OUT

A caption for identification connected with its identifying part by means of a line or arrow.

CAPTION

A title or heading.

COLOR SEPARATION

The term applied to art work to be printed in color, but prepared in outline or solid blacks or specially colored acetate sheets. Generally each of these is prepared on a separate sheet of acetate, for each color desired, in the printing.

COMBINATION PLATE

A printing plate on which both halftone and line art are reproduced.

COMPOSITE

A pasteup of two or more photographs or pieces of art work.

CONTACT PRINT

A photograph printed in direct contact with a negative and therefore the same size as the negative.

COPY

May refer either to text material used in an advertisement or to art work or photography used for reproduction.

CROP MARKS

Short straight lines used by the artist to indicate a section of a photograph or art work which is to be reproduced.

CROPPING

The selection of an area within a photograph or drawing utilized for reproduction.

DROPOUT

A term indicating that the white areas are to remain in the art work in the printed stage.

ENGRAVER

A person or firm involved in making letter press plates for printing.

EDITORIAL ART

Art work used for books, magazines, or newspapers for illustrating factual or fiction material as compared with advertising material.

FRENCH FOLD

A printed form in which the sheet is folded once halfway and then again halfway at right angles across the original fold.

GRAPHIC ART

This may refer to the general field of art related to printing.

HALFTONE

This may refer either to art work which is made up of actual gradations of tone as compared with solid black or solid colors, or it may refer to the plate used to print such art work.

ILLUSTRATION BOARD

A cardboard on which thin white paper is mounted for art work.

KEY DRAWING

A drawing prepared for color separation to which other colors may be conveniently registered, or indicated on overlays.

LAYOUT

A rough pencil or color sketch indicating the design or form which an editorial or advertising page will assume.

LIGHTBOX

A glass covered box containing an electric light over which a photograph or drawing may be placed for tracing.

LINE ART

Art work which is composed only of solid black or solid colors. See term "Halftone" for comparison.

LINE CUT

The printing plate made from line art.

MECHANICAL

The term applied to art work which is usually an assemblage of various units such as photographs, type proofs, etc., with or without overlays of other material, and which will be used for reproduction.

OVERLAY

Art work or an indication on tracing paper, bond paper, or acetate, placed over other art work to be printed in combination with it, or used as a guide by the printer.

PLATE MAKER

A general term referring to the person making a letter press, lithographic, or gravure printing plate.

PROOF

A sample of the initial printing of art or type submitted to the client for approval before the finished printing is done. "Reproduction proof" refers to type carefully printed on good paper stock for paste up on a mechanical to be used for reproduction.

PRE-SEPARATED ART:

See Color Separation.

REGISTER MARK

A fine line cross mark usually enclosed in a circle used on art work to enable the plate maker and printer to register the various plates when printing.

REPRODUCTION

The printed version of art, photography or type — whether it be letter press, lithography, gravure or silk screen.

REVERSE LETTERING

White lettering on a gray, black or colored background.

SCALING

The process of determining what will be the new proportional dimensions of artwork when it is reduced or enlarged.

SCREEN

A sheet of glass with fine lines scored at right angles to each other, from 55 to 185 lines per inch. Artwork and photographs are photocopied through this screen for halftone reproduction.

SEPARATION

The difference in value which separates an image from its background or another image.

SILHOUETTE

An art or photographic image against a white background.

SQUARE HALFTONE

A reproduction of artwork wherein there is a slight tone over the white areas and the lines are broken up by the halftone screen. See "Combination plate" for comparison.

TRIM MARK

Short straight lines indicating where the page is to be cut for trimming the printed art to specified size.

TYPE PROOF

See "Proof".

TYPOGRAPHER

The person or firm which sets type for printing.

VELOX

A photographic print made from a line or screened negative, generally used for reproduction.